TED TURNER SPEAKS

Insight

from the

World's Greatest

Maverick

~ ✸ ~

TED TURNER SPEAKS

SPEAKS

Insight

from the

World's Greatest

Maverick

~ ✳ ~

JANET LOWE

John Wiley & Sons, Inc.

New York • Chichester • Weinheim • Brisbane • Singapore • Toronto

> This book has not been prepared, approved, licensed, or endorsed by
> Ted Turner.

Library of Congress Cataloging-in-Publication Data:

Lowe, Janet
 Ted Turner speaks: insight from the world's greatest maverick /
by Janet Lowe.
    p.   cm.
 Includes bibliographical references.
 ISBN 0-471-34563-6 (cloth : alk. paper)
 1. Turner, Ted. 2. Businesspeople—United States—Biography. 3. Tele-
communication—United States—Biography. 4. Sports team owners—
United States—Biography. 5. Sailors—United States—Biography.
 I. Lowe, Janet. II. Title.
HC102.5.T86 A5 1999   384.55'5'092—dc21
 [B]   99-042193

Book design and composition by Anne Scatto / PIXEL PRESS

Printed in the United States of America

10 9 8 7 6 5 4 3 2 1

~ ✳ ~

*This book is dedicated
to Emmet and Judith Wolfe,
great friends who prove
that sailing and baseball are
a powerful combination.*

~ ✳ ~

CONTENTS

PREFACE

"If Ted Turner were a color, it would be red—the red of the surface of the sun," said Reese Schonfeld, the founding president of Turner's world-altering television experiment, Cable News Network (CNN).[1]

Robert Edward Turner III—empire builder; creator of the Superstation concept; founder of CNN and a half-dozen other cable television channels; four-times Yachtsman of the Year and winner of the prestigious America's Cup sea race; environmentalist; peacemonger and avid philanthropist—surely is one of the world's most original but confounding billionaires.

Among his various nicknames; the Capsize Kid, for spending so much time overboard when he was learning to sail; The Pirate from Peachtree, for the way he found cheap or free programming and walked off with the market shares of networks; Captain Courageous, after one of his yachts; Captain Outrageous, for the dumbfounding things he says and does; and Captain Comeback, for Turner's miraculous rebound from a business deal with MGM/UA that nearly bankrupted him. Turner is most frequently dubbed the Mouth of the South, a description that does not please him.

Along with William S. Paley and David Sarnoff, Turner has been called one of the three most important figures in television broadcasting.

But all those descriptions aren't quite enough. Without using government funds, public opinion surveys, focus groups, or consultants, Turner transformed news coverage from either local or national reporting to global news gathering. In constructing his media empire, Turner followed his own counsel, took risk after risk, met challenge after challenge, and dozens of times seemed on the brink of defeat. Yet he persevered far beyond the point where money or power was the motive for his actions.

Turner's story is riddled with contradictions, but one thing is sure. He doesn't fit in to any standard-size box. Through his indomitable will and drive, he has shown himself capable of remarkable open-mindedness, growth, and change.

• An advertising man who avoided the news because it depressed him, Turner created the first 24-hour, global news channel, changing both journalism and world diplomacy forever.

• A longtime Republican, Turner also is an environmentalist who favors nuclear disarmament, a women's right to reproductive choice, and other liberal concepts.

- Kicked out of Brown University for raucous behavior, Turner later was forgiven and inducted into Brown's athletic hall of fame and was granted an honorary doctorate.

- Although Turner is an aggressive talker capable of grandiose statements and exaggerations, most of his associates claim that he speaks honestly and acts with integrity.

- Well-known for driving modest cars, keeping his family on a tight budget, and paying low salaries at his television operations, Turner poured $1.7 million into a campaign to win the America's Cup.

- Deciding he had almost everything he needed in life, in 1998 Turner presented one-third of his fortune—$1 billion—to the United Nations.

These are only a few of the Turner surprises. The chapters ahead will address many more. Although he has offended one group of citizens after another, Turner has tweaked America's, and even the world's, imagination.

Turner has been honored many times, by Harvard University, the Radio-Television News Directors Association, the Urban League of Atlanta, and even *GQ* magazine. Turner was named *Time* magazine's 1991 Man of the Year. Charles Lindbergh, Franklin Roosevelt, Winston Churchill, Adolf Hitler, Joseph Stalin, and Madame Chiang Kai-shek are among those who have received the award since it was first given in 1927. Barbara Walters interviewed him for her 1995 *10 Most Fascinating People* show, and *People* magazine named him among "The 25 Most Intriguing People."

Yachtsman Dennis Conner (who in 1980 beat Ted out for the right to represent the United States in the America's Cup race) said he got to know Turner better when, in 1973, Turner asked Conner to be on his America's Cup crew.

"Once you get close to Ted, you've got to appreciate him if only because of his exuberance that sometimes borders on wildness. You don't have to be around him long before you know all about him, because he's so wide open and talkative. I sometimes think that he would have been more at home as a Civil War cavalry leader (Confederate, of course)—I can just see him leading a charge."[2]

It would be prudent for readers to take some of the things Turner says with a rather large dose of salt: He talks a lot, and not all of his comments are meant to be serious or even accurate, although he invariably says exactly what's on his mind at the moment.

Example: In 1988 Turner spoke at a breakfast seminar in New York City put on by the Center for Communications. Robert Wright, president of NBC was there, as were the chief executive officers of MGM/UA, Time Inc. Magazine Group, and several hundred members of the press. Each speaker gave a short but upbeat summary of the outlook for his particular medium. Turner, speaking twice as loud as necessary, said: "Cable has grown incredibly. . . . It is already twice as valuable as all the broadcast stations and networks put together. . . .The top nine cable networks are profitable right now. . . .Only one broadcast network is profitable. . . . In the next five years, the value of the cable industry will go from $100 billion to $200 billion."

At this point the moderator interrupted Turner "Where did you get the $200 billion figure?" Turner, exasperated, barked, "I dreamed it up! Just now!"[3]

But remember, added Ted, "We dreamed this whole industry up."[4]

Turner usually talks with his mind in overdrive, without considering the consequences of his words. How does he get away with it?

Roger Vaughan, a boat racing writer who met Turner over forty years ago when they were both students at Brown, identified the quality that allows people to overlook Turner's nerve-rattling words and actions: "Turner has always had a quality, an unfailing sense of the absurd that certain lucky people are born with, which underlies everything he does. It is this which makes Turner likable, even enjoyable, despite his basic racist tendencies, his chauvinist approach to women, his elitist view of society, and his fascist political ideology."[5]

Example: During training for an America's Cup race, Turner launched into one of his spontaneous prattles: "You know, I can do anything I want. If I wanted to walk from there across to that boat [he pointed over a stretch of ocean water] I could do it. Weeeell, let's just assume I could. . . ." Then Turner laughed uproariously with his audience.[6]

Despite the good-old-boy, common-man facade, Turner is well educated, a student of classic literature from an early age. He claims he isn't an accountant, but he is quick to see the long-term profit potential in ragged assets, untested new technology, and unusual business situations. He is a shrewd judge of character, hiring capable people who tend to stay with his companies for decades.

Porter Bibb, a former correspondent for *Newsweek* who wrote a book about Turner, says: "He developed this persona as a teenager, as a wise-cracking, loud-mouthed idiot's delight, but in reality he is none of that at all. He is very cerebral and a man of deep moral convictions."[7]

"The biggest misconception about Ted is that he shoots from the hip," said Alan F. Horn, chairman and chief executive of Castle Rock Entertainment. "The opposite is true. He gives a tremendous amount of thought to things. Before he does something, he takes all the right steps he's supposed to take and is as careful as the most conservative businessman in America."

Turner has worked extremely hard to break new ground and become a billionaire and world opinion leader. A glance at the timeline at the end of the book, which runs from Turner's birth to the present, reveals a schedule that would have exhausted almost anyone else in the world by now.

"If you look back at the people who have changed the American life-style," said media analyst William Donnelly, "you find they're people like Ted Turner. His kind of energy, integrity and willingness to take risks are very hard to come by. They're exactly what is missing today in America."[8]

These traits are rare, to be sure, but not missing. *Ted Turner Speaks* is the seventh book in the Speaks series. Earlier subjects were superinvestor Warren Buffett; revolutionary General Electric chairman Jack Welch; software entrepreneur Bill Gates; talk show host Oprah Winfrey; basketball legend Michael Jordan; and revered evangelist Billy Graham. Each of these contemporary Americans shares something with Ted Turner. They are the premier performers in their field. They are the yardsticks by which others worldwide are measured. Most important, each of these people changed their world forever and, in doing so, has left a personal mark. Ted Turner, like each of the others in the Speaks series, knew early in his life what he would do. He never varied from his vision, always holding deep faith in his own abilities and ideas. Thanks to the men and women in this series, other nations still look to the United States for fresh and effective ideas and the ability to implement change.

Some aspects of Turner's influence have been accidental, by-products of his main goals. A Saudi Arabian friend claims that Turner has had tremendous impact on the women's rights movement globally, simply by having women on the air, presenting programs on CNN Headline News and CNN Worldwide. "Just the fact that women in my country see women working in television gives them the idea that they too could do something," he explained.

~

Every effort has been made to verify all the quotations in this book, and the footnotes will show the sources from which these comments are taken. Some extremely vivid stories have been left out because they could not be verified.

Many stories circulate about Turner's unruly behavior, especially during the early part of his life— racist remarks, verbal abusiveness to his wives and children, excessive competitiveness. Some are well documented, and Turner himself does not deny them. Many cannot be excused, but they are part of his life story. While I have acknowledged the truth about Turner, I also have tried to describe the complexity of the truth. He has struggled with both external and internal demons, and while he does not seem to have fully conquered his wild tendencies, his family, friends, and business associates report that there has been progress.

Love him or hate him, Ted Turner is a man to be reckoned with. For all the pain and suffering he has endured, all that he has inflicted, he lives life right up to the limit. Whenever he occasionally flips over the edge, his grinning face soon appears at the rim, and he hauls himself back and starts again.

You might say of Turner, the odds are good but the goods are odd.

This book has been one of the most challenging in the *Speaks* series yet one of the most hilarious. I hope you enjoy reading it as much as I've enjoyed working on the project.

Janet Lowe
Del Mar, California
JUNE 1999

ACKNOWLEDGMENTS

Much of the credit for preparation of this book goes to Austin Lynas, my husband and helpmate. Many thanks to Myles Thompson, Jennifer Pincott, Robin Goldstein, and the staff at John Wiley & Sons; my literary representative Alice Fried Martell; Emmet and Judith Wolfe, for their inspiration and input; Phyllis Kenney, for her administrative assistance; and Jolene Crowley, for taking care of many matters while I was buried in research and writing.

TED TURNER SPEAKS

Insight

from the

World's Greatest

Maverick

~ ✳ ~

LESSONS
FROM SAILING

FASTNET

When Ted Turner's father committed suicide at age 53—in the midst of a business crisis—and his teenage sister died a year later, death became Turner's comrade-in-arms. He lived his life taunting death, literally in his yachting adventures and symbolically in his business ventures. Turner spoke of death often as a young man and railed against the terrible legacy left to him by his father. But after the brutal British Isles Fastnet yacht race of 1979, Turner was clearly established as a survivor.

The Fastnet race is an absolute test of endurance and skill in the best of circumstances, but in 1979 a sudden, fearful storm blew in from the North Atlantic and before the event was over, 23 competitors died, 21 boats were destroyed, and another 30 were severely damaged. As Turner and his crew battled through raging gales and towering waves toward the finish, they were unaware of the fate of their fellow racers. For several hours it seemed to the outside world that

Turner was lost at sea. But in the end he sailed out of the maelstrom, soaked to the skin, with his mouth running like a circus barker, spewing his blunt opinions to a stunned British audience. After a mistaken announcement that another boat had won, Turner was declared the victor in the most competitive yacht race in the world.

> *"It's no use crying. The king is dead. Long live the king. It had to happen sooner or later. You ought to be thankful there are storms like that, or you'd all be speaking Spanish."*[1]

With his usual lack of subtlety, Turner suggested that it was a storm, rather than the efforts of Queen Elizabeth I's fleet, that fended off a Spanish invasion of England in 1588. It is a fact, however, that the dreadful storm that finished off the already defeated Spanish Armada has gone down in history.

∼

Despite his bewildering remarks, the tragedy laid to rest any suspicion Turner was a loudmouth dilettante who succeeded by mere luck. This storm was not survived by luck alone. Turner entered the race in a sound boat and with an experienced and trusted crew who held a steady course through harrowing circumstances.

> *"You're supposed to have a strong vessel with crew and equipment for any condition. I feel a little like*

Noah. I knew that the flood was coming and I had a boat ready that would get me through it."[2]

Turner was at the helm of his 61-foot-yacht, *Tenacious*, his second boat with that name. To add to the tension, Turner's young son Teddy was aboard as a crew member.

~

"Like any experience, whenever you come through it you feel better. We're not talking about the other people who died, but to be able to face it all and come through it is exhilarating."[3]

~

"Sailing in rough weather is what the sport is all about."[4]

~

Turner dismissed the accusation that he was more concerned with winning than with the fate of the sailors who drowned:

"No, I was very concerned about my fellow yachtsmen who drowned. I went to the memorial service and we sang the seaman's hymn: O heavenly Father strong, hear us when we cry to thee for those in peril of the sea."

~

Turner soon realized his comments seemed harsh, but a combination of adrenaline, exhilaration, and horror compelled him to try to talk his way out of the verbal quagmire:

> *"Aw, it—it's hard to be real happy today, because so many people have gone up to that great yacht race in the sky. But at least they won't have to worry about setting the storm trysail anymore. In a way, I'll be happy when my turn comes, too."[5]*

$\sim$

Turner hoped that some good would come of the calamity.

> *"It will draw attention to the problem. We are making boats too skimpy, too lightly built and too lightly rigged. I have been predicting something like this was going to happen. The Western states took no notice when Hitler was advancing, and everyone laughed at Noah when he was building the Ark. It takes a disaster like this to make people take notice."[6]*

KEEP GOING

Turner once explained how to win a yacht race: "You just have to keep going."[7]

$\sim$

When surveying his sailing trophies, Turner told a friend: "Anyone could have done it if they had the money and the imagination. We started out and just kept going. Like Alexander. He started out to beat the Persians and kept going until he conquered the whole world."[8]

~

"If Christopher Columbus had a southern accent, then I'd be the man."[9]

~

"The first time I went to Europe [in 1966], I sailed across on a little 38-foot boat. We didn't do a lot of sleeping. It took 20 days and nights. Six-man crew, two men on a watch. We weren't really set up for that long a race because of a lack of provisioning. We ran out of water. We went on rations. We had to reconstitute our dehydrated food with salt water. It was pretty rough. We were down to basic survival conditions. When you're racing across the ocean on a small sailboat, dodging icebergs and killer whales, you live at a subsistence level, you know. I mean, it's hard to eat, you're wet a lot of the time and just going to the bathroom is a chore."[10]

~

Terry McGuirk, who was a senior executive at Turner Broadcasting System, said that Turner applies the "just keep going" philosophy to business. "His vision and the guts to stick to the vision drive the company."[11]

~

In 1986 Turner observed: "I've already met or exceeded all goals for personal wealth and accomplishment. Nothing ever comes easy—my first eight years of sailing I didn't even win my club championship. But I just

5

kept working and working and working—that's the secret of my success. Now I'm like a runner who has kept running and running and one day finds he has run the Boston Marathon. I don't need to be the best anymore, I'm just part of a team. I'm just widening, broadening."[12]

~

It may be an urban legend, but as the story goes, one day in the 1970s Turner was dashing down the main street of Anderson, South Carolina, hurrying to a business meeting. Suddenly he was smacked by a car, but Turner was so preoccupied with the sales pitch he was about to make that he bounced off, jumped up, and kept on running.[13]

FIGHT LIKE AN UNDERDOG

Both in sailing and in the business world, Turner seems most comfortable when cast as the underdog. He told his 1977 America's Cup crew: "We need to win, because we're just a bunch of bums. Are there any bluebloods here? Raise your hands. None. I didn't think so. Anybody from fancy prep schools? Awright. We could have won it with the latest in computers, but that's not our style. We like to slug it out. These other guys are going to have to slug it out with a bunch of streetfighters from the Bronx and Queens."[14]

Not exactly from the Bronx and Queens, Turner

nevertheless fired up the crew. Though they weren't native sons of the prestigious New York Yacht Club, home of the America's Cup, Turner graduated from McCallie, one of the most respected schools for boys in the South, and he and several crew members attended Ivy League colleges.

~

After winning the Southern Ocean Racing Circuit series in 1966, Turner explained that there were many elements to successful sailing. However:

"You can't win races without working harder than the other guys."[15]

~

Despite his reputation for winning, Turner has been a legitimate underdog, in sailing and in life. In 1977 Turner won the Congressional Cup, a match race held at the Long Beach Yacht Club in Southern California. It was his eighth attempt to win the race.

DEMAND THE BEST AND GET IT

Author Roger Vaughan said that the boating community should have known Turner would win the America's Cup: "Had they ever spent a night at sea with [Turner], engaged in a race with unseen boats, working under the lash of his Captain Bligh tongue, they couldn't have doubted. Turner at sea is a splendid executive, a man who works his crew just less than himself, a man who demands and gets the teamwork and precision that wins races."[16]

∼

America's Cup champion Dennis Conner noted: "Ted's strong point is neither innate ability nor attention to detail and preparation—it is his enthusiastic competitiveness and leadership ability. He drives himself and his crew as hard as men can be pushed."[17]

∼

Turner was infamous for getting excited, yelling at his crew, then launching into a coughing fit. He sometimes coughed so hard he would spit up blood.[18]

In the 1978 Newport race, Wally Stenhouse, a fiftyish experienced sailor in excellent physical condition, was handling the mainsheet on Turner's yacht *Tenacious*. Turner apparently didn't think Stenhouse was working fast enough. "Get that geriatric case off the main and find someone who can trim it," Turner shrieked. Like most people who sail with Turner, Stenhouse simply ignored the harangue and continued to work. Despite Turner's reputation for verbal abuse, every crew member who sailed with him during the 1977 America's Cup sailed with him again in 1980.[19]

∼

To Turner, the verbal rantings were just a way to release tension:

"When I sailed a Finn and wasn't doing well, every-body used to say I cussed my crew. I'd talk to my-self: 'You stupid son-of-a-gun, you. You can hike out harder.'"[20]

〜

"You have to be a gentleman, and you have to do what is expected of you on the water as well as off."[21]

NOTE: For times when Turner was not as much of a gentleman, see the section "Sorry, Sorry, Sorry."

〜

"Ted is always winning, never losing," said Bunky Helfrich, an old friend and regular member of Turner's sailing crew. "And he gives that same feeling to people sailing or working with him."[22]

〜

Legaré Van Ness, one of Turner's America's Cup crewmen, explained why Turner had such a steady following, especially among his sailing crew. "It's mainly because Turner is loyal to his crew. He is a winner, and that's important too, but loyalty is the main thing."[23]

〜

As he prepared for the 1977 America's Cup, Turner observed: "All I know is I get what I want. Maybe because I want things more than others do. I wanted my television stations on the satellite, and there it is. I wanted to win the America's Cup and that's getting close. I wanted to be worth $50 million and in a few years it might be double that. People love me, all over the place, they really do. I can communicate on all levels."[24]

HAVE NO FEAR

Turner once told a fellow sailor: "Your problem is that you are too worried about losing. There is no disgrace in losing. Everybody loses from time to time. Don't worry about it."[25]

~

"Exposure to defeat is a very important thing. Anyone who doesn't look to get beaten is doing a disservice to himself. You have to go where the hot stuff is and get whipped."[26]

~

"I'm like the grass. I get tramped down one day and spring right up the next. I've been beaten so much that one more loss doesn't make any difference. Losing is simply learning how to win."[27]

~

Turner was once asked if he was afraid of the sea:

"Afraid of the sea? I thought I was going to go under a few times, but I wouldn't say I'm afraid of it. I have a tremendous amount of respect for it, but the

10

worst thing that can happen to you is that you'll die and that's going to happen to all of us anyway, so there's no point in sitting around and worrying about it. The coward dies a thousand times, a brave man but once."[28]

～

Turner has said when yacht racing in a heavy wind: "Put the spinnaker up and let God take it down."[29]

～

Turner refuses to let fear control either his life on the sea or in the business world: During an interview with *Sport* magazine in 1980, Turner was asked what starting CNN would cost:

Turner: "Fifty million. But I intend to be in the black."

Sport: "When?"

Turner: "Before I go broke."

Sport: "When will that be?"

Turner: "Hopefully before I run out of my ability to raise additional funds or to generate them on the Superstation or through some other sleight of hand, the same way I made it through the Fastnet race. When the smoke cleared and the storm blew away, there we were and that's how I'm going to be when this is over, hopefully. And if not, I'll be blown away.

Sport: "Do you worry about that?"

Turner: "Nah. A little bit. But I'm going to be blown away sooner or later. At least I'm doing what I enjoy and what I think is right. If the Cable News Network doesn't work, I'm broke."[30]

～

Turner suggested there might be an advantage to losing all of his money:

"At least I wouldn't have to worry about all these problems. And nobody would interview me any more, thank God. It might not be a million dollars, but I could make enough to feed my family. I was in the U.S. Coast Guard making $87 a month and cleaning latrines. They gave me all the latrines to clean. I cleaned them pretty good. They gave me an honorable discharge."[31]

～

Turner's frequent comments about death, especially early in his life, seemed to border on obsession: "If I have to make a quick turn in a car," said former TBS executive Robert Wussler, "he'll get all tensed up and yell, 'You're gonna kill me, we're not gonna make it!' He's always talking about death, about the possibility of some terrorist walking in and pumping bullets into him."[32]

～

Turner recognized that an outspoken, wealthy, and influential person takes a risk with his life:

"Someday, somebody will put a bullet in me. I would really like to stay around for a while, but I really do believe that I'll be assassinated."[33]

THAT'S THE SPIRIT

"For Ted," said Robert Wussler, "the glass is never half empty or half full—it is always three-quarters full."[34]

~

"Don't stop just because you're little and you're afraid and it looks like you haven't got a chance. The rabbit can get away from the fox, but he better get on his hind legs and hop."[35]

~

"I just love it when people say I can't do something. There's nothing that makes me feel better, because all my life people have said I wasn't going to make it."[36]

~

Turner was asked what is the secret of his proven motivational skills:

"It's mental attitude. You know, there are a whole lot of little slogans—be sure you're right and then go ahead—either lead, follow, or get out of the way— get with the problem—don't stand around beefing, pick something up and carry it away."[37]

~

Turner spoke at the 1978 Cable Television Convention:

> *"You have to have a little balls. Hell, I've got 'em or I wouldn't be here."*[38]

IT'S TRYING THAT COUNTS

"My desire to excel borders on the unhealthy."[39]

~

"I've got a larger dose of motivation than most people have. Some people are born fleet of foot, make great runners. When basic characteristics were doled out, I got more than my share of competitiveness. That's probably all. In fact, it may not be all that healthy."[40]

~

"In college there was no reason that I should end up winning the America's Cup more than any of the other good sailors. But I went out and made it to the top. I went into the real world and went to work. I worked 18 hours a day. I moved with speed. I plotted, schemed, and planned, and did crazy things. . . . When you're little you have to do crazy things, you can't just copy the big guys. To succeed you have to be innovative."[41]

~

Sid Pike, general manager of Turner's television station, said of his boss: "He has a tremendous desire to win. He doesn't like to lose. And if he does, he is one of the few people I have ever known who benefits from the loss. Ted asks himself, 'Why did I lose?' I don't know why he has to win so much. It's a compulsion with him."[42]

∽

In the 1974 America's Cup trials, Turner lost big, despite his syndicate's costly, custom-made boat *Mariner*. Why did Turner return in 1977 and try again?

"Because for years I have had to prove myself in increasing circles of competition. The reason I have to do this is my latent inferiority complex, and frankly, I am beginning to think the whole deal is full of crap."[43]

∽

"I really wonder whether or not too much emphasis is placed on success. I think it's overrated. The average person realizes that it's hardly worth making the effort to get to the top. They take it easy and have a good time, play softball. To get to the Olympics as a swimmer you have to swim eight hours a day for 15 years. Then what have you got? Prune skin from too many pools. You have no chance to date, to get to know people. It's crazy."[44]

~

"I don't think winning is everything. It's a big mistake when you say that. I think trying to win is what counts."[45]

~

"All of my life I've had this gnawing pain that I might not succeed. It is only in the past four or five years that I have put that ghost to rest."[46]

AMERICA'S CUP

Ted Turner saw his first America's Cup race in the late 1950s, when he and a college chum visited Newport, Rhode Island. The two watched *Columbia* defend the cup against the British boat *Sceptre*.

"We were on a sail boat about thirty feet long owned by the family of a friend of mine. We were near Castle Hill, and they towed the boats by—both white, if I remember. The crews were all big, muscular men, with their matching shirts on. I'm sure that at the time I didn't just decide I was going out and win the Cup, but I was pretty impressed."[47]

~

The New York Yacht Club gained possession of the original Hundred Guinea Cup (now called America's Cup) in June 1851, when the yacht *America* defeated all 14 boats of the Royal Yacht Squadron in a transatlantic race. For years the event was little known out-side Eastern yacht racing circles.

America's Cup has become sailboat racing's most prestigious trophy. It is presented to the winner of a match-race series between 12-meter boats (best of seven races). The challenge generally is given every three to four years, and traditionally the race takes place in the Atlantic Ocean off Newport, although in recent years it also has been sailed in the Pacific near San Diego, California, and in the waters off Australia.

The America's Cup is a closed-course race run near the coast, as compared to the Southern Ocean Racing Circuit (SORC), which is an open ocean race. While the Fastnet race is a contest of guts and glory, the America's Cup has evolved into a race in which victory depends on high-priced, high-technology equipment.

Defending the America's Cup is a team effort, financed by a syndicate of wealthy backers. The syndicate chooses a manager, designer, builder, and skipper.

The America's Cup is a lyrical, lovely game for the wealthy, people like Reynolds Du Pont of Delaware and Texas billionaire Perry Bass, although teams often employ other highly skilled sailors to give their team the competitive advantage.

Team members devote six months for practice time and the race itself. Often they have spent months, even years, training for the event by participating in other sailing matches.

The New York Yacht Club was edgy about admitting Turner to membership, but it did so to permit the clearly dedicated yachtsman to participate in the 1974 race.

George Hinman, manager of the syndicate that financed Turner's first run at the America's Cup, said he had reservations about taking Turner on as skipper: "I spoke with just about everyone who Ted ever sailed with, and those who have sailed against him, and the reports were all good. The problem seems to be that he was a bad boy ashore. So I talked with him like a Dutch uncle. He is a fine person who matures a little more each year."[48]

Due to difficulties with the newly designed *Mariner*, Turner's first attempt to win the America's Cup ended ignominiously. His boat was eliminated in an early round.

～

Despite problems with his newly acquired Atlanta Braves baseball team, Turner tried again in 1977. He returned to the race with a new syndicate, a different boat, but many of the same crew members.

Although Turner had an uneasy relationship with domineering and bombastic Lee Loomis, the manager of the *Courageous* syndicate, the two men kept their differences at a minimum. The only visible problem occurred when Turner reportedly made a scene at a restaurant, and Loomis insisted that he write a letter of apology to the club.

NOTE: For more on this incident, turn to the section "Sorry, Sorry, Sorry."

Turner had several public rows with Lowell North, a San Diego sailmaker. Turner felt North had promised to sell him sails for *Courageous*, but North felt he should sell only to the *Enterprise*, a boat with which North was involved. Ultimately, the sails didn't matter.

Turner and his crew handled their boat and the sea brilliantly and preserved the America's Cup for the New York Yacht Club. After winning the 1977 America's Cup challenge, Turner said: "There will never be a time in my life as good as this time. I can't believe all this is really happening to me. I'm so hot I just tell my guys to stand by me with their umbrellas turned upside down to catch the stuff that falls off me and onto them."[49]

⌣

"Sometimes I think my father is somewhere watching all this. Watching me make the big time. I wish he could come back and see, you know? Like the father in Carousel? *The dead father, when he comes back to see his daughter at graduation? Damn! We were good friends. I wish my father could be back just for a day."[50]*

⌣

When Turner and his crew returned to help defend the Cup in 1980, the story was far different. *Courageous* by then was an old boat, which didn't seem to bother Turner.

"It's kind of like having an old wife. A devil you know is sometimes better than a devil you don't. At least we know we've got a good boat."[51]

Nevertheless, Turner was preoccupied with the launch of CNN, and the cruel whisper "Ted is dead" spread around Newport. Turner and his crew didn't even qualify for the main event. The loss apparently was painful for the excessively competitive Turner, but he may have realized that the time had come to choose between his business aspirations and his sailing life. Turner also was saddened by the fact that the America's Cup had become so cutthroat. It was now apparent that money was a major element in winning the race. Turner's group spent $1.7 million to win America's Cup in 1977, but Turner spent only $400,000 in 1980, when he was beaten by Dennis Conner.[52]

~

Turner complained that America's Cup had lost its charm:

"There is a lot of unsportsmanlike conduct in this series which I don't like. Commercialism. I'm putting stuff into this sport. They're taking it out."[53]

He snapped: "My men have to work for a living. I guess I'm the last of the amateur sailors. Can you imagine. Dennis [Conner] sailed 340 days last year ... him a fully grown man!"[54]

A few months later he told a reporter: "I'm through with sailing! I don't even want to talk about it. I'm sick of sailing! I'm sick of the professionalism, the downright cheating. Did you read about the

SORC last winter? All three winners were disqualified! They broke the rules. I'm through with all that!"[55]

Later, when asked in the mid-1980s he didn't race America's Cup any more, Turner replied that he'd "grown up" since those days.[56]

～

Turner said that he quit yacht racing when it was no longer fun. Yet he's also said that he wouldn't have missed the experience of yachting for anything:

"In reflecting on what yachting means to me, I guess I would have to start with the sheer beauty of the sea and the water, the wind and the clouds, the gulls and other sea birds—the general beauty of the whole thing has been most enjoyable.

"Next would come the many fine shipmates, comrades and competitors from all over the world whom I met during those years, and the friendships that resulted.

"Then would be the thrill of the competition and the tremendous efforts we put forth. Then, of course, there is the excitement . . . the excitement of facing squalls or getting on a plane in a Flying Dutchman or flying along at 20 knots in a Hobie Cat."[57]

～

Turner survived many hair-raising moments as a sailor, but he did pay a price for years at sea—skin cancer. Turner addressed the 1994 graduating class of

Georgia State University, just before he was scheduled to undergo surgery:

> *"The one piece of advice I can give you is put on sun screen and wear a hat."*[58]

HAVE FUN

"The most fun that you ever have as a man is in doing men's things. Men's things are primarily getting a bunch of guys together and going out and conquering a country, fighting a war, winning a big fight, putting a baseball team together."[59]

⌒

Turner recalled a pep talk he gave to his baseball team, the Atlanta Braves: "I told them a story about something that happened in 1977, when I won the America's Cup. We won most of our races in June, then lost most of our races in July. After the last race in July, everyone was writing us off. I remember a reporter asked me: 'How are you going to approach the finals?' I told the team my answer to that question: 'I'm going to have fun. I'm going to enjoy myself.' I told the Braves to do the same thing: 'Have fun. Enjoy yourselves. Don't worry about everything.'"[60]

⌒

"To me business is a game. It's like a poker game: You're playing for chips, but the most fun is the game. I may look like a clown, doing flips at a baseball game, but I'm a very deadly serious person in trying to accomplish things just for the satisfaction of accomplishing them. Struggling hard to achieve something is the most fun I get. All my life is a game. Everything is a game—and you keep score with dollars, to a degree. It's like there are two kinds of

points. *I consider the money like hits in a baseball game. They're great, but the runs are what really count. And the runs are just being successful and having a good time."*[61]

～

"People have the most fun when they're busting their ass."[62]

A SCARED, SCRAPPY KID

ED'S BOY

It is easier to understand Ted Turner when you know something about his father. Both in life and death, Ed Turner's shadow has loomed over his son's life:

> *"My father could be absolutely charming or he could be a horse's ass. He could be the kindest, warmest, most wonderful person in the whole world, and then go into a bar, get drunk, and get into a fist-fight with the whole place."*[1]

Ed Turner was brought up in Sumner, Mississippi, the son of a prosperous Mississippi land and store owner who fell on hard times during the Great Depression. When money became scarce, Ed Turner left school and migrated north to Cincinnati to find work. There he met and married Ted's mother, Florence.

Ted was three years old when his father joined the Navy, and his parents took off with his infant sister for a series of World War II military posts. Ted was left with his grandmother in Cincinnati. When he was just six, he was enrolled in a boarding school. He spent his summers with his grandmother in Ohio or with his paternal grandparents on their Mississippi farm.

Ted loved his grandparents' cotton farm, where he spent hour upon hour outdoors, just messing around, exploring, catching frogs, and doing the typical things that country boys do. It gave Turner a lifelong love of nature.[2]

~

Ted Turner inherited his mother's good looks and outgoing personality—and his father's extreme mood swings and driven nature.[3] Turner's parents were a mix of European heritage:

> *"I got my thrift from the Scots, my work ethic from the Germans, and my colorfulness from the French and the British. My judgment and conservatism come from the Dutch, and the Irish—well, the Irish, they're all off their rockers, unbalanced."*[4]

~

Turner's mother insisted that her son's competitive spirit had come from his father. "He certainly doesn't get it from me," she said. "I never cared if I won or lost."[5]

~

It was Ed Turner's conviction that Ted should fear his father—and thus respect him—and that Ted should feel insecure—and thus become more competitive.[6]

Turner's first wife, Judy Nye, said of Ed Turner, "He believed insecurity bred greatness."[7]

~

Ted lived with his family for only one year of his schooling. His parents often argued about how to raise Ted, according to Florence Turner: "Teddy was a little on the mischievous side, but he was never really bad. His daddy just ruled with an iron hand. Ninety percent of the arguments I had with Ed were over his beating Ted too hard."[8]

~

Turner says that on one occasion when he did something really bad, his dad ordered Ted to beat him: "He laid down on the bed and gave me the razor strap and he said, 'Hit me harder.' And that hurt me more than getting the beating myself. I couldn't do it. I just broke down and cried."[9]

~

"He told me all the time he loved me. We were real close. He was my best friend. He was best man at my first wedding. I was crazy about him even though he drove me nuts from time to time."[10]

~

In his mid-thirties, Turner still suffered conflicting feelings over his relationship with his late father:

> *"There's always the possibility, I don't think there really is one, but there's a possibility of an afterlife, and my father always expected a lot from me and he could be very hard on me at times, and just in case there is an afterlife, I just don't want him bugging me for the rest of eternity. You know, I'd like for him to say 'a job well done' if and when I see him there because I just don't think I could take it. It was hard enough, you know, growing up as a boy and then a young lad; I couldn't take that kind of treatment for the rest of eternity."[11]*

⁓

In 1981 Ted Turner was in the middle of a speech, when he suddenly stopped and raised over his head a copy of *Success* magazine with his face on the cover. Ted gazed up at the ceiling and whispered: "Is this enough for you, Dad?"[12]

⁓

Being featured on magazine covers did not subdue Turner's drive to achieve. Several years later Jimmy Brown, the houseman whom Turner says practically brought him up, observed: "Right now Mr. Ted is doing the same thing his daddy did. He's working himself to death."[13]

THE TERRIBLE CADET

At age six, Ted Turner was sent to military school.

> *"My father had this burning desire to succeed. Success, success, success! And I went to this military school where they pounded in 'You got to get to the top, boy, you got to get to the top.' Well, I got to the top."*[14]

~

When Ted was nine, the Turners moved to Savannah, Georgia. Ed Turner decided his son needed more discipline than he was getting at his Cincinnati school and enrolled him in the rigid Georgia Military Academy. Ted arrived late in the semester and stood out from his classmates because of his Yankee accent. He soon was entangled in a series of fights with the other boys:

> *"I was from Ohio. I was a northerner. I don't know what it was. Yes, I do know what it was. The other kids thought I was a show-off and a smart ass."*[15]

~

After the family moved to a house on Abercorn Street, just a few blocks from the city's historic old Oglethorpe Square district in Savannah, Turner first attended Charles Ellis, the local public school, the Home of the Bobcats.[16]

Turner's mother wanted him to continue to live at home and attend the local school, but his father felt that mothers spoiled sons and sent the boy off to

McCallie School, a Presbyterian military academy in Chattanooga, Tennessee. Among McCallie's other alumni are Pat Robertson, founder of the Christian Broadcasting Network, and James Killian, former president of Massachusetts Institute of Technology.

"Ted hated McCallie," his mother said. "He was a devil there. I had to buy him new shoes every time he came home. He wore them out walking punishment tours."[17]

~

While at McCallie, Turner bet his classmates that he could catch three squirrels by the end of the day. Hundreds of the bushy rodents scurried the grounds, but nobody believed Turner would be able to catch one, let alone three. All took the wager.

After spreading black shoe polish over the trunk of an old oak tree where dozens of squirrels lived, Turner lit the tree afire, causing thick black smoke to rise into the branches. One by one squirrels jumped from the tree, right into a basket held by Ted, who immediately began collecting on his bet.[18]

~

An inordinately energetic and independent kid, it took some time for Ted to settle down at McCallie, and Turner admits he was a terrible cadet in the beginning:

"But then, I turned it around. I'd been the worst cadet, and I was determined to be the best."[19]

~

His classmates and professors describe Ted as a self-contained youngster who operated by his own rules. Turner kept a dish with dirt under his bunk, where he grew grass, which he clipped with manicure scissors. He loved rescuing wildlife, taking in birds, squirrels, and all sorts of small animals.[20]

Ted was a great reader, and pored over ancient fables and Greek and Roman tales of gods and heroism. He read C. S. Forester and Joseph Conrad and studied the exploits of Admiral Nelson and other maritime heroes. As he grew older and learned to sail, he enjoyed *Men Against the Sea, Mutiny on the Bounty*, and other seafaring adventure books. His personal model, for a time, was Alexander the Great, the Macedonian king and conqueror.

> *"As much as I hate war now, I was basically a warrior. I was reading about war all the time as a kid. Fighting and soldiers and all that stuff. What I wanted to be was Horatio, Admiral Nelson, Napoleon, Alexander the Great and Pericles; they were the greatest warriors."*[21]

> *"I was interested in one thing, and that was finding out what you could accomplish if you really tried. My interest was always in why people did the things they did, and what causes people to rise to glorious heights."*[22]

As a teenager, Turner wrote a poem called *Indecision*:

"At the feet of Hannibal / Then Like a ripe plum Rome once lay / Oft he put the time of conquest / To a later, better day.... Pretty strong, huh?"[23]

~

"As a kid, I was a little bit of an artist and a poet. I painted and sculpted a little, but it was too slow moving for me to really get into. But the whole idea of grand things always turned me on. The grand idea of building the Parthenon. And it was a grand idea to build the pyramids. I'm inspired by the great works of the past and the present. I like all that stuff. When I went to Paris, I saw the Louvre, you know, and I've been to Versailles."[24]

~

At the end of his first year at McCallie, Turner had to stay on several extra days to march off all the demerits he'd earned. When he was barely old enough to join a work crew, his father assigned him a job, $50 a week, to work on the labor gangs that erected and maintained the roadside signboards. Furthermore, Ted was expected to pay $25 for room and board at home. When Ted rankled at the rent, his father challenged him to find another place to stay if he thought he could get a better deal.[25]

~

Turner says that while he certainly was bright enough in school, he could not be considered brilliant:

"The highest I ever did on an I.Q. test was 128, but I have some 115s (scores), too. That puts me in the 95th to 97th percentile."[26]

～

Turner's sons attended both McCallie, which is no longer a military school, and The Citadel (a Charleston, South Carolina, school famous for its difficulties in switching from an all-male to a coeducational institution). Turner has donated large sums of money to both schools.

When he was 54, Turner addressed the McCallie student body:

"I love this school a lot. It did a lot of good for me. . . . A lot of times you don't appreciate things as much when you are there as when you have the opportunity to look back on them from a number of years."[27]

～

"I thought the education I got here was terrific. I learned to think for the first time."[28]

JIMMY BROWN

"My father worked a lot, and didn't spend much time with me. I was really raised by this black man."[29]

～

Jimmy Brown is a Black Gullah from the Isle of Hope, Georgia. The Gullah people are celebrated for maintaining their African heritage and integrating it into a unique New World language, culture, and cuisine all their own. Despite a congenitally withered right arm, Brown went to work for Ed Turner when he was 17 years old to take care of Turner's Great Lakes schooner, *Thistle.* Later Brown was responsible for the Turner's motorized yacht, *Merry Jane.* Brown served three generations of Turners as houseman, chauffeur, bodyguard, and baby-sitter.

"I was brought up in the old school," said Brown. "Hard work. Good manners. And faith in God."

~

Perhaps most important of all, Brown taught Ted Turner to sail, hunt, and fish.

"The boy didn't take to it at first," Brown recalled. "I'd say, 'Mister Ted, let's go exploring.' We'd go off to different islands, fish, hunt. That's when he started sailing, as a way to get there."[30]

~

Turner says Jimmy Brown is ". . . like a second father to me, like a big brother. I didn't have any brothers and we just hit it off from the very beginning. My dad encouraged it because he was very close to Jim too. He was an employee but he was like part of the family."[31]

~

"It's an Uncle Remus—type relationship. That's the way it is. I love him like my own father. You can say

he's a servant if you want to, but I don't think of him like a servant."³²

～

"I would clearly say my friendship with Jimmy Brown has made me a great believer in equal rights and equality for all people."³³

～

"Ted Turner's not a prejudiced person," says Jimmy Brown. "If you can do the job, you have it. What else can you say about a man?"³⁴

～

Brown and Turner remain very close. Brown supervised the Turner children, who lived on a sailboat of their own during the America's Cup races. He was best man at Turner's wedding to Jane Fonda. Brown attends the family Christmas celebration in Florida and their July 4th gathering in Montana.

Jimmy Brown is a millionaire now, thanks to his early investment in Turner's company stock.

THE CAPSIZE KID

Ed Turner bought Ted a small boat and encouraged him to race. Sailing soon became a passion with the boy. At 11, Ted entered the junior Penguin races at the Savannah Yacht Club. His first year he capsized 11 times. By his third and fourth year of racing, he placed second in the club championships. During the summers he was home from boarding school, Ted spent the hours he wasn't working honing his sailing skills.

> *"I didn't have a lot of natural athletic ability. This was a game that took nerves and brains and heart. And I had a lot of heart."*[35]

~

> *"Actually, I was a lousy athlete. In school I fumbled around with just about everything—wrestling, boxing, football, kickball, baseball, basketball, track. But I really wasn't coordinated or fast. Besides, to do a good job at something you've got to concentrate in one area, not be a jock-of-all-trades. Sailing was something I could do."*[36]

A CLASSICAL EDUCATION

When Turner graduated from McCallie in 1956, he hoped to seek admission to the U.S. Naval Academy at Annapolis. His father insisted on an Ivy League school instead. After being turned down by Harvard, Ted enrolled at Brown University in Providence, Rhode Island.[37]

~

Turner went to Brown at 17, tall, good-looking, with a combination of Southern charm and Turner brashness. He introduced himself to his roommates as the world's best sailor and world's best lover. Not surprisingly, he didn't pay much attention to his studies. Classmate Doug Woodring recalled, "He was just going to shoot for a C average and have the time of his life, which he pretty much did."[38]

~

College was Ted's first experience in living outside a controlled, even protected school environment. To complicate matters, life was unsettled at home. His sister, Mary Jane, suffered from a cruel terminal illness and his parents were divorcing. All of these elements seemed to bring out Ted's wildest behavior. He reportedly painted swastikas on the doors of Jewish students and Ku Klux Klan warnings on the doors of black students. Ted was kicked out of Kappa Sigma, his fraternity, for burning down the frat's homecoming display. According to reports, he sometimes cocked his .22 rifle and fired it from his dorm window, which was a few hundred yards from the office of the school president in University Hall.[39]

~

Some of the tales of Turner seem to have grown to mythical proportions. He has denied the story that while attending Brown he sent a bowling ball down the Thayer Street bus tunnel.

"That's not true. I don't bowl."[40]

~

One of Turner's greatest distinctions at Brown was serving as vice president of the Debating Union, although he received the most honors for his activities on the sailing team.

Ted was named commodore of the Brown Yacht Club and co-captain with Bud Webster of Brown's sailing team. The team made it to the national sailing championship in Newport Harbor, California, where Brown finished fifth place.[41]

~

Yachting writer Roger Vaughan met Turner at Brown, where they both belonged to the university's yacht club. Vaughan described Turner as too redneck, too boozy, and too loud for the historic eastern school, but Turner endeared himself to Vaughan because he won a lot of boating races. "Brown's racing sailors drank as much as they won in those days, and they won regularly," wrote Vaughan. "But even among such an alcoholic lot, Turner was a standout. It wasn't that he drank so much more than anyone else, he was just more spectacular about it."[42]

~

Although his father had a business career in mind for his son, Ted chose to major in the classics. Supposedly this was an easy major area of study at Brown, but it was consistent with Turner's earlier passion for classical and heroic literature. Why not go one step further and study the classics in their original languages?

Ted's choice enraged his father so much that Ed Turner wrote a letter to his son in protest. In retaliation, the young Turner had the letter published—anonymously, with no mention of the Turner name anywhere—in the college newspaper, *Brown Daily Herald*. The letter leaves little doubt about where Ted got his strong opinions and colorful manner of speech:

My dear son:

I am appalled, even horrified, that you have adopted Classics as a Major. As a matter of fact, I almost puked on my way home today. I suppose that I am old-fashioned enough to believe that the purpose of an education is to enable one to develop a community of interest with his fellow men, to learn to know them, and learn how to get along with them. In order to do this, of course, he must learn what motivates them, and how to impel them to be pleased with the objectives and desires.

I am a practical man, and for the life of me I cannot possibly understand why you should wish to speak Greek. With whom will you communicate in Greek? I have read, in recent years, the deliberations of Plato and Aristotle, and was interested . . . in the kind of civilization that would permit such useless deliberation. Then I got to thinking that it wasn't so amazing after all, they thought like we did, because my Hereford cows today are very similar to those ten or twenty generations ago. I am amazed that you would adopt Plato and Aristotle as a vocation for several months when it might make pleasant and enjoyable reading to you in your leisure time as relaxation at a later date. For the life of me, I cannot understand why you should be vitally interested in informing yourself about the influence of the Classics on English literature. It is not necessary for you to know how to make a gun in order to know how to use it. It would seem to be that it would be enough to learn English literature without going into what influence this or that ancient mythology might have upon it. As for Greek literature, the history of Roman and Greek churches, and the art of those eras, it would seem to me that you would be much better off learning something about contemporary literature and writings, and things that might have some meaning to you with people with whom you are to associate.

These subjects might give you a community of interest with an isolated few impractical dreamers, and a select group of college professors. God forbid!

It would seem to me that what you wish to do is to establish a community of interest with as many people as you possibly can. With people who are moving, who are doing things, and who have an interesting, not a decadent, outlook.

I suppose everybody has to be a snob of some sort, and I suppose you will feel that you are distinguishing yourself from the herd by becoming a Classical snob. I can see you drifting into a bar, belting down a few, turning around to the guy on the stool next to you—a contemporary billboard baron from Podunk, Iowa—and saying, "Well, what do you think about old Leonidas?"

. . . There is no question but this type of useless information will distinguish you, set you apart from the doers of the world. If I leave you enough money, you can retire to an ivory tower, and contemplate the rest of your days the influence that the hieroglyphics of prehistoric man had upon the writings of William Faulkner. Incidentally, he was a contemporary of mine in Mississippi. We speak the same language—whores, sluts, strong words, and strong deeds.

It isn't really important what I think. It's important what you wish to do with your life. I just wish I could feel that the influence of those oddball professors and the ivory towers were developing you into the kind of man we can both be proud of. I am quite sure that we both will be pleased and delighted when I introduce you to some friend of mine and say, "This is my son. He speaks Greek."

. . . In my opinion, it won't do much to help you learn to get along with people in this world. I think you are rapidly becoming a jackass, and the sooner you get out of that filthy atmosphere, the better it will suit me.

Oh, I know that everybody says that a college education is a must. Well, I console myself by saying that everybody said the world was square, except Columbus. You go ahead and go with the world, and I'll go it alone. . . .

I hope I am right. You are in the hands of the Philistines, and damn it, I sent you there. I am sorry.

Devotedly, Dad[43]

Florence Turner said her son apparently published his father's letter because he was angry that his father had flown to Reno, Nevada, to get a quickie divorce. It was at this time that Ted started drinking seriously. Before then, said his mother, he wouldn't so much as have rum sauce on ice cream.[44]

~

Turner's father promised to give him $5,000 if he did not drink liquor until his twenty-first birthday. Ted didn't make it. He followed in his father's footsteps and developed a reputation as a hard drinker. But one of his drinking exploits was nothing but trickery. Turner bet his fraternity brothers that he could down an entire fifth of whiskey without stopping or passing out. After the contest, Turner immediately went to the bathroom and started throwing up. Before chuga-lugging the fifth, Turner had swallowed nearly a pint of olive oil, thus lining his stomach so that the alcohol could not be absorbed. Turner liked to gamble, especially when he had some secret advantage.[45]

~

Following his parents' divorce, his mother got custody of Ted's dying sister, and Ted was assigned to live with his father, although Ted was 18 years old and could have been considered independent. Visits home became difficult, especially since his father went on regular drinking binges. The younger Turner continued to spend most of his holidays and summers working in the billboard business and sailing.

~

Turner attended Brown before the advent of the birth control pill and before the women's movement began. Behavior codes, especially those relating to sex, were strictly enforced. The first time Turner was placed on suspension was for a semester for a panty raid on a women's dorm at nearby Wheaton Women's College. He spent the suspension meeting part of his military obligation with a six-month tour with the U.S. Coast Guard. He then returned to school for his junior year.

~

By then Turner had acquiesced to his father's wishes and switched to economics as a major, but he barely passed his courses.

"When I got into economics I began running into commie professors who thought everybody ought to work for the government. I was opposed to that and defended the free-enterprise system to the extent I almost flunked the course. To me the capitalist system is still the best way to get things done.... what a great system!"[46]

~

His father successfully drove Turner away from the classics as a course of study, but Ted's favorite professor at Brown, John Workman, said Ted's heart was still with the Greeks.

"We lost Ted in a sense," said Workman. "He changed to economics. But we didn't really lose him. He was still around. The real humanist will always go out of his way to be different."[47]

~

Turner was booted out of college for good after entertaining a girl in his dorm room.

"At Brown I was a rebel ahead of my time, I got thrown out of college for having a girl in my room. Today they have girls and guys living in the same dorm."[48]

~

Years later Turner dreamed of getting revenge on the administrator who dismissed him:

"I was going to go piss on his grave when I heard he died, but there hasn't been time. For a while I consid-

*ered sending it [Ted's urine] to Providence in a bot-
tle and having someone pour it on for me, but I never
got to that."[49]*

~

Although Turner caused the university a lot of grief
and never graduated, eventually all was forgiven. He
was awarded an honorary doctorate by Brown in 1993.

When Turner spoke at the school, Brown Univer-
sity President Gregorian introduced him as "One of
Brown's truly great sons, and the husband of Jane
Fonda."[50]

~

His dismissal was the end of Ted's formal education
but not the end of his youthful escapades.

Turner and a school pal went on a search for inde-
pendence to Miami, Florida. There they planned to
work and play but had great difficulty finding jobs,
especially at a salary that would support their drinking and partying. Luckily, Turner discovered he still
owed some time to the Coast Guard, so he reported
for his final tour of duty.

During his Coast Guard stint, Ted proposed marriage to his first wife, Judy Nye. He then returned
home to Savannah, where he again went to work for
his father. Ed Turner served as best man at the wedding, which would be the last happy event before the
Turner family's lives went off on a course of pain and
sadness.

FROM MISSIONARY TO MADMAN

Ted Turner received Bible training at McCallie and thought highly of his Bible teacher. Ted decided he wanted to be a missionary.

> *"Religion was pounded into us so much that I was saved seven or eight times."*[51]

~

All that changed when his beloved younger sister, Mary Jane, developed lupus at age 11, and suffered from the disease and its complications for many years before she died in 1960. Turner recalls:

> *"She was sweet as a little button, she worshiped the ground I walked on, and I loved her. A horrible illness."*[52]

~

When Ted's young sister died, he seemed to lose his faith in God.[53]

> *"Prior to [her death] I was very religious."*[54]

~

Turner once called Christianity ". . . a religion for losers."[55]

~

> *"I don't think I'd like to go to heaven. I just can't see myself sittin' on a cloud and playin' a harp day in and day out."*[56]

~

Although his interest in a church-oriented career faded, Turner never lost his missionary zeal.[57]

"I think that there's a battle going on in the world between the forces of good and the forces of evil and I want to be damn sure that the forces of evil don't win and there's a good chance that they may. I think we're at the crossroads between the potential of living in the garden of Eden or the battle of Armageddon."[58]

~

When asked who he really is, Turner once responded: "Charlemagne, saving Christendom from the infidels."[59]

THE BRIEF GOOD-BYE

Peter Dames spent a lot of time with the Turner family after he and Ted left Brown University. Dames said Ed Turner cut a theatrical swath. "He might meet you out front of the house in a silk robe or maybe a white linen suit with a mint julep in one hand," said Dames. "Sometimes he drank Scotch from the bottle. There was duck hunting, and barbecues, lots of food and drink. He really knew how to do it. He was a great host. He laid the red carpet out for us. I think he was happy Ted had finished with Brown."[60]

~

In 1962 Ed Turner and a group of investors acquired General Outdoor Advertising and split up the company among themselves. In return for cash and a secured note totaling $4 million, Turner took control of General Outdoor's operations in Atlanta, Norfolk, Richmond, and Roanoke. This made his company the biggest billboard firm in the South. But Ed Turner also was involved in a personal battle to stop smoking and drinking. That, along with the added responsibility and debt load, put him under a great deal of pressure.[61]

Convinced that he made a dreadful mistake, Turner sold key parts of his firm to several friends in the business, then retreated to his plantation to commit an act that would haunt his son all of his life.

Turner's father, at age 53, blew his brains out with a .38-caliber pistol at the family's South Carolina plantation, Binden. For all his erratic and harsh behavior, Ed Turner apparently loved his son, and clearly Ted knew that he did. Yet Ed Turner's suicide left Ted with a heartache that could never be resolved:

> *"That left me alone, because I had counted on him to make the judgment of whether or not I was a success."*[62]

~

Turner's stepbrother, Marshall Hartman, suspected that Ed Turner suffered from a bipolar, or manic-depressive, condition, an ailment that few people recognized in the 1960s. "I'd say it was probably impossible for anybody to deal with Ed when he was on one of his extreme highs or lows," said Hartman. "I guess the same could hold for Ted. He was just the mirror image of his father, and the two of them were always going at each other, tooth and nail."[63]

～

Turner told Diane Sawyer, during a *60 Minutes* television interview: "If I had one wish for something that would give me personal joy and satisfaction, it would be to have my father come back and show him around. I'd like to show him the whole shooting match. . . . I really would. I think he'd really enjoy it."[64]

～

One reporter asked Ted if he ever reflected on his father's suicide:

"I refuse to answer any questions about things that happened 23 years ago. It's a waste of time. I don't think about the past, I think about the future. Go on, you got 20 more minutes, next question. Let's talk about the Goodwill Games. I should be working right now, not frigging around with you. I'm sick of stories about me. Part of me wishes no one ever heard of me. I'd have some privacy, I wouldn't be bugged to death by you. No, I wish I had time to reflect. I'm involved in such an intensive series of negotiations and business deals none of my mental powers can be spent reflecting. Do I miss it? No, I don't have time to miss it. Now more than ever is the time to act. . . . It's 10 o'clock. Goodbye. . . . Uh, good luck with your story. Do you need any more time with me?"[65]

IT'S ADVERTISING, STUPID

LEARN AS YOU GO

Ted Turner was a teenager when he began working at his father's billboard business, doing hard physical labor in the blazing southern summer sun.

> *"But it's fun too, getting up at five in the morning to get out and install a new sign before the traffic gets started. And painting billboards, you're Michelangelo in the Sistine Chapel, except that you don't have to work lying on your back."[1]*

~

Turner was living by his often-proclaimed motto:

> *"Early to bed, early to rise, work like hell and advertise."[2]*

~

Turner started out in the advertising business and has spent most of his life in some form of advertising. He simply changed media, moving from billboards, to radio stations, to UFH television, to satellite-distributed television networks. In each case, the trick has been to build a communications vehicle for which more ads could be sold at higher prices.

~

In 1963 Ted said persistence was his secret to success in the signboard industry:

> *"I'd like to point out that we're tenacious, we don't accept marginal locations. We pick the location that we want and then keep going back until we get it. In fact, we literally hound the people to death in a nice way. Personally, I've had people throw up their hands after forty hours with them on about thirty calls and say, 'OK, OK.'"[3]*

~

To an audience of women at a luncheon to woo advertisers, Ted described the lengths to which he was willing to go to sell ads:

> *"My Daddy said, 'If advertisers want a blow job, you get down on your knees.'"[4]*

~

Shortly after he married Judy Nye, Turner's father sent him to Macon, Georgia, to become general manager of the Turner Advertising operation there. Working long hours and six and a half days a week, Ted doubled sales in Macon in less than two years. He joined the Rotary Club, chaired a Red Cross fund-raising drive, and immersed himself in the young businessmen's community.

~

Turner once said that in some ways, he misses those early days:

"I'd like to be back in sales, but they've kicked me upstairs to a nice corner office. I try and keep up with it. My secretary gets me the sales reports, which makes me feel like [Bill] Paley in his final years at CBS."[5]

~

By the time Turner's father ended his own life, Ted knew a lot about the outdoor advertising business. He'd worked eight summers with the billboard crews and two years as manager in Macon.

~

Ed Turner demanded such high performance from his son that shortly before his father's death, Ted declared: "You're not leaving the business to me. You're leaving me to the business."[6]

Ed Turner said he'd never thought of it that way. But that is the way it turned out.

ACCEPT NO LIMITS

When Ed Turner took his own life, it shocked his 24-year-old son, but it also gave Ted an incentive, something to focus his life on. Ted did not agree that his father was overextended financially and had pleaded with Ed not to sell valuable segments of what had become the largest billboard company in the region.

When he inherited Turner Advertising, Ted decided to reverse the sale and put the company back together. The fact he didn't have much of a background in deal making did not deter him.

Perhaps hoping for some latitude because the buyers had been friends of his father, Turner explained that Ed Turner had made a rash decision while suffering a nervous breakdown. He petitioned the buyers to cancel the sale. When they refused, Turner set to work to do whatever was necessary to prevent the sale from going through.

Ted was prepared to go to court and ask that the contract be nullified because his father was not in his right mind when he signed the deal. In the meantime, using the part of the company he still controlled, Turner jumped billboard leases by hiring away the leasing department from the sold segment of the company—a common franchise-stealing trick in the billboard business. He threatened to delay the sale and let the business run down, burn records, and generally debilitate the company.

Turner was determined to keep Turner Advertising intact and finally prevailed upon the buyers to back away. They did, however, require Turner to pay an extra $200,000 to retrieve the business, and if he ever defaulted on a debt payment, they had the option of stepping in and seizing the company. Turner agreed, even though he didn't have enough money to meet their demands. Turner began selling every asset that he could and dredged up cash from every possible source. At the same time he was relentless in negotiating the terms of the deal, and eventually, because of tax considerations, he was granted seven years to pay the repurchase price.

> *"I was sad, pissed, and determined. I was only a kid, but I had learned how to hustle. I went out and convinced the employees to buy stock in the company. I sold off all the real estate that I possibly could to raise cash. I sold my father's plantation. I borrowed against our accounts receivable. I squeezed the juice out of everything."*[7]

~

An early business partner, James Roddy, said that "His salvaging of that company with big sharks biting at his heels was the finest proof of the pudding. He rallied his people and he worked like hell. That may have been his finest hour."[8]

~

Once Turner figured he had a handle on the billboard business, he didn't stop there. Next he bought a rundown radio station in Chattanooga, where he'd gone to school. He changed the format, used his own billboards for promotion, and turned the station around. Soon he bought a second station in Chattanooga, two in Charleston, and one in Jacksonville, Florida. All were scraggly properties, but he bought them cheap and fixed them up.[9]

~

Irwin Mazo, Ted's chief financial officer in the early years, was amazed at what he saw happen.

"I watched Ted put his father's business in order," said Mazo. "He did that with his eyes closed, with plenty of time on the side for his sailing. He could have retired anytime during those early years and never looked back. But then we started making acquisitions, always trying to use the other guy's money. That was Ted's genius. He could charm the pants off anybody when he wanted to. Usually the fellow we acquired would turn right around and work twice as hard for Ted as he ever had for himself."[10]

~

Turner once described his financing techniques this way: "What you do is you get a bank, and you borrow all you can borrow."

In fact: "You borrow so much they can't foreclose on you."[11]

Turner was on his way to becoming a global media mogul.

THE BRAT WHO
ATE ATLANTA

REDEFINING THE QUESTION

Ted Turner's media career started when he purchased several ragtag radio stations around the South and made them profitable. When he bought the nearly defunct Atlanta UHF station, WRJR Channel 17 in 1970, Turner began to pick up momentum. By merging Turner Communications Corporation with Rice Broadcasting, he gained control of the television outlet that in time became the Atlanta Superstation WTBS. He traded $2.5 million in his company's stock for a battered, badly run, low-frequency station that was losing $600,000 a year.

NOTE: The same year he bought Channel 17, Turner sailed in several major yacht races and was named Yachtsman of the Year.

~

The station's call letters were changed to WTCG, for Turner Communications Group, and Turner went to work fixing it up. Turner resurrected the approach he used as a 17-year-old kid at the Tennessee State Debating Championship. He reinterpreted the question in a way that nobody else had thought of and were unprepared to debate. Rather than striving to look like a dignified network channel, Turner gave viewers an alternative. He took a station that was in danger of going bankrupt, then found cheap, easy, escapist entertainment to broadcast. He promoted the station on his unleased signboards, then started selling ads like mad.

∼

Because the station had little to offer national advertisers, in the early days most of the commercials promoted direct mail companies. TV shoppers sent their checks for Ginzu knives and country and western audiotapes to the Atlanta station. In a crude form of market analysis, Turner piled up the mail by location to find out where his viewers were.

> *"It wasn't exactly a compelling argument to Procter & Gamble, but I thought it was pretty cool."[1]*

∼

In addition to the demographic information, Turner noticed something else—on every twentieth letter, the stamp had not been canceled by the post office:

> *"Hey, I said, here's a chance to make some revenue. I took the letters to our mail room and made them cut off and re-use the stamps. I figured I made a dime on every stamp."[2]*

~

The FCC required that Channel 17 run 40 minutes of news, and Turner ran just the minimum, a spoofy, low-budget, rip-and-read news program that aired only in the middle of the night. Turner hated gloomy news, so in an effort to make people laugh, his anchorman once read the entire program while holding a photograph of Walter Cronkite in front of his face. On another occasion the anchor wore a gorilla outfit while reading a story of a guerrilla attack. He added a German shepherd as his coanchor. Peanut butter was spread on the dog's lips just before airtime, and as the dog licked it off, a voice-over recording of Cronkite was played to make it look like the dog was talking.

In addition to wrestling and roller derbies, Turner broadcast lots of situation comedy reruns. In fact, he took pride in the reruns as a community service:

> "Gomer Pyle *is a program that stresses values. I mean he was always doing something nice. He came out on top all the time, even though Sergeant Carter was always giving him trouble. Gomer Pyle is pro-social! The typical network mentality is to be number one in the ratings irregardless of what you have to do, and that's why so much sex, violence, antisocial behavior, and stupidity has taken over the networks. The networks should put a disclaimer on their product, saying, 'Watching this is dangerous to your mental health.'"[3]*

Years afterward Turner expressed nostalgia for some of WTCG's reruns:

> *"I liked TV better years ago, I'd like to bring shows like those shows back on television. Shows like . . .* Playhouse 90, The Andy Griffith Show, The Waltons, Little House on the Prairie. *Families on the air. Programs weren't as antisocial as they are now. You know the saying, you are what you eat? Well, don't you think you are what you see? Television had a higher quality fifteen years ago."*[4]

Turner continued: "You know, you can take children and you can either turn them into eagle scouts or Hitler Youth. What you've got today are a trashy, snotty bunch. Television determines their central character."[5]

~

> *"Every now and then, the networks do something decent, but mostly they bring us Mr. Whipple squeezing toilet paper and Charlie's Angels in their underwear. People watch these shows, but people take cocaine too. That doesn't make it right. The networks make heroes out of criminals! They're worse than the Mafia!"*[6]

~

Turner took the first step to creating the original Superstation by engaging in opportunistic television. When a network station declined to rerun *Star Wars*,

Turner nabbed it. When the NBC affiliate decided not to run network shows, Turner signed those on and plastered his billboards with the announcement that NBC had come to Channel 17.

~

Turner made it a policy to gain ownership of material whenever he could, believing this was the key to success:

"We control more of our own software than any other programming entity in the world. We're really in the business of remarketing product. We buy as much software as we can, and find as many ways to get it out there."[7]

Delighted with the success of his bargain-hunted station and its patchwork programming, Turner took the next step toward creating the Superstation concept by using microwave and cable television technology to sell Channel 17—and its commercials—in geographically distant markets:

"I'm going after the networks!"[8]

~

"I give [the networks] hell because they don't serve the public interest. They look at the viewer the same way a slaughterhouse looks at its pigs and cattle. They sell them by the pound to the advertiser—the same way they sell ham hocks and spareribs."[9]

~

GOING TO THE MOVIES

Always a film buff, Ted Turner personally hosted the Sunday afternoon classic movie on Channel 17:

> *"I used to sit in a big wing-back chair and introduce the Sunday morning Academy Award Theater. I enjoyed it and it was great during those winters I was off sailing in Australia. The kids could turn on the set and see their daddy at Christmas. But I really didn't have the time to do it."*[10]

Turner claims to have watched the Orson Welles classic movie *Citizen Kane* more than 100 times. What was so appealing about the fictional Kane (said to be modeled after newspaper baron William Randolph Hearst)? Both were separated from their families as children, and in *Citizen Kane* there was the hint that Kane's mother allowed him to be taken from the family because the boy's father beat him harshly. Both Kane and Turner built media empires and had frustrating and failed relationships with their wives. But equally important, both Kane and Turner had ample opportunity to become members of the conservative, wealthy, and powerful establishment—but both held themselves apart as the underdog outsider.

The parallels between Kane and Turner were striking early in Ted's life, but Turner seems to have outgrown the compulsion to be an outsider. Kane died an isolated and lonely old man, while Turner's relationships with family members improve as he grows older.

"I like the romance of the Confederacy, you know, going down against overwhelming odds. I liked Rhett Butler in Gone With the Wind, *because he was trying to help a lost cause. Like when I bought the Atlanta Hawks."[11]*

Although Turner assumes a Rhett Butler demeanor (he even named one of his sons Rhett), his life suggests that he takes many of his cues from Scarlett O'Hara. Self-absorbed and used to getting his own way, Turner rose again and again from the ashes of failure. Scarlett swore that she would never be hungry again. While Turner has spent little time being physically hungry, he has been haunted by a lingering Southern sense of loss and deprivation that has driven him to accumulate enormous wealth. And like Scarlett, in recent years Turner seems to believe that the only thing that lasts is land.

NOTE: For more on this, see the section "Give Me Land, Lots of Land."

During the 1977 America's Cup challenge, Turner made a speech at a Brown University football team fund raiser:

"I'll tell you what, if you haven't seen MacArthur, *it's an old man's movie, it's pretty good, even if you didn't like* MacArthur. *I went to see it last night to get pumped up, and it did pump me up. Sport and good sportsmanship and doing your best are the*

most important things any man can learn in his life. The friendships you make in good competition and everything, well, you can't beat it anywhere. . . ."[12]

～

In 1986 Turner bought most of the assets of Metro Goldwyn Mayer/United Artists, primarily to get possession of the studio's film library.

When he tried to colorize that film library to make it more appealing on cable TV, the film community rose up in protest. Director John Huston, Woody Allen, and Jimmy Stewart were among those who called the modernization a travesty against art. Turner didn't understand their problem:

"Women put on makeup, don't they? That's coloring, isn't it? Nothing wrong with that. Besides, when was the last time anyone took photos in black and white? I know, Ansel Adams—but he's dead too."[13]

～

Turner yearned to own a movie studio and finally got his wish. In 1993, for $1 billion, he bought two small film companies. The first, New Line Cinema, is a solidly profitable B-movie outfit with a couple of very lucrative franchises, such as Freddy Krueger and the "Nightmare on Elm Street" series and the Teenage Mutant Ninja Turtles titles.

The second, Castle Rock Entertainment, is a top-of-the-line studio founded by a quintet of Hollywood insiders, including actor/director Rob Reiner. Castle Rock's lighthouse logo has become familiar to movie fans everywhere as a result of its hits *A Few Good Men*, *City Slickers*, *The Shawshank Redemption*, and many others.[14]

~

Since Turner's purchase, both New Line and Castle Rock have produced many award-winning movies.

> *"I hope to be a major force in the movie business. I love movies."*[15]

~

Even with the purchase of the movie companies, Turner wasn't done acquiring media properties:

> *"I've been through a lot of campaigns. I'm only 54, but I've already got the mileage of a 150-year-old man. I'm like a New York City taxicab that has three drivers driving 24 hours a day, seven days a week. I'm still pretty tough. I'm still building this company. I haven't done everything I want to do."*[16]

Something of a ham, Turner has even acted on the screen. In *Gettysburg*, Turner Pictures' $20 million, four-hour Civil War epic, Ted appears in a one-line cameo as a Confederate soldier who gets killed.

I WAS CABLE WHEN CABLE WASN'T COOL

Playing on the title of a popular country western-song, Turner once posed for a poster wearing cowboy clothes, holding a guitar: "I was cable when cable wasn't cool."[17]

~

The first television cable is believed to have been laid in 1949, when appliance dealer John Watson put a TV antenna on a mountaintop and hooked it up to his television by a cable. He then offered to connect anyone who purchased a television set to his antenna.

In the early years, Turner transmitted Channel 17 beyond Atlanta and into secondary markets by use of microwave dishes, which transmitted the signal to local cable providers like Watson. But microwave transmission was slow, expensive, and didn't travel far.

Two things made it possible for Turner to transform his small UHF station into a Superstation. In 1975 the Federal Communications Commission lifted some of the rules that had restricted cable television growth. That same year RCA launched its first communications satellite. Turner's great stroke of brilliance was realizing the technological advantages afforded by satellite broadcast. Satellites could rapidly and easily relay television signals to any area of the globe covered by the orbiting electronic gnomes.[18]

~

On several occasions, Turner testified before congressional committees on the importance of revising laws and regulations related to television. Sometimes he was persuasive when communicating with elected officials, sometimes he was not.

In 1982 Turner and his lawyer met with Senator Slade Gordon and an aide in Gordon's Washington office the day before hearings on new cable television regulations. No sooner had Turner arrived than he launched into a diatribe against lawyers in general. Suddenly the tirade ended and Turner asked:

"Are you a lawyer, Senator?"

Turner's lawyer stepped in with the answer. "He was the attorney general of the state of Washington for ten years."

"Guess that's the same thing," said Turner.

Turner continued ranting for another 15 minutes, then suddenly bent over, put his head in his lawyer's lap, and said to the senator:

"Okay, your turn now."

Minutes later Turner got up and left while the senator was still talking. When the door slammed shut, the senator's aide said, "How can that man be in charge of a television network? He's a maniac."[19]

～

"Satellite. That was the big step. I'm like the bear that went over the mountain to see what he could see. One thing opened up another, and I kept moving on. Remember, I went from a small sailboat on Lake Lanier to the America's Cup."[20]

～

On December 27, 1976, Turner began national transmission when he launched "The Superstation that Serves the Nation." When WTCG (later WTBS) first beamed its signal to RCA's Satcom 1 satellite full time, the station's coverage was instantly increased to well over 10 million square miles. Before then, Turner's small station had a broadcast range of 45 miles on a good day.

∽

As usual, Turner's motivation for broadcasting nationwide was to create a medium that would attract national advertisers, one that would allow him to charge higher ad rates because of the greater number of potential viewers. But the Superstation was a new concept, and Turner knew it might be a tough sell:

> *"I knew it was going to be hard to convince the New York advertising community, but I had no idea how hard. My first team of salesmen ended up like the soldiers in the opening scene of* Saving *Private Ryan. They were mowed down to a man."[21]*

∽

In time, advertisers were attracted by the prospect of reaching Turner's 7 million viewers in places as far-flung as Atlanta, Oklahoma, and Alaska.

∽

A *Business Week* writer explained why Turner was able to convince advertisers to try an untested medium:

"Turner never said: 'We are cable.' He simply sold his services as TV delivery systems that would help you reach audiences that the network had lost. That meant advertisers didn't have to worry about it being a new medium and maybe not working."[22]

~

Turner's new enterprise was a clear threat to the networks, which had a grip on national television audiences and, thus, national ad revenues:

"The networks are in stark terror of us."[23]

~

When Turner first moved to Atlanta to run Turner Advertising and then bought Channel 17, few Georgians saw these as particularly momentous events. But on his fortieth birthday, in 1978, Atlanta had a glimmering of how Turner's enterprises would come to dominate and even define their city. A group of Ted's friends produced a birthday video of his life entitled *The Brat Who Ate Atlanta.*

~

Several years later an interviewer asked Turner, "What do you think you have accomplished for the good of mankind?"

Ted's reply was right on the mark: "Well, I'm only 44. I think I'm just getting started."[24]

SEIZE THE TECHNOLOGY

CHANGING TELEVISION FOREVER

"I remember being at a baseball game with Ted," recalled New York Yankees owner George Steinbrenner. "There was a group of us, and he was saying he wanted to broadcast the news all day long because he had to wait until 6 and 11 to get the news. I said to myself, 'What the hell is he talking about?' But damn if he didn't do it."[1]

~

In 1980 Ted Turner proclaimed: "I can do more today in communications than any conqueror ever could have done. I want to be the hero of my country. I want to get it back to the principles that made us good. Television has led us, in the last 25 years, down the path of destruction. I intend to turn it around before it is too late. And the hour *is* late."[2]

~

When Turner decided to create the first 24-hour news network, Cable News Network, he put his entire bankroll on the line. But he felt the cause was just:

> *"Back in the Dark Ages, only the church and politicians had knowledge, and the people were kept in the dark. Information is power. I see CNN as the democratization of information."[3]*

~

Fred Friendly, president of CBS News, had little doubt that Turner's Cable News Network would rewrite television rules forever. "Right now, the networks operate in virtually a closed market," said Friendly, "but Ted Turner will make the public realize that the market can open up. He will be the link to TV's future."[4]

~

Not only was Turner looking for an unfilled niche in the cable TV business, he believed that news presentation could and should be better:

> *"In their race for ratings, their newscasts dig up the most sordid things that human beings do, or the biggest disasters, and try to make them seem as exciting as possible. In their entertainment programs, they make heroes of criminals and glamorize violence. They've polluted our minds and our children's minds. I think they're almost guilty of manslaughter."[5]*

～

"Look, it's not the government's fault that we have the disastrous situation that we do inflation-wise, balance of payment-wise, military-wise, it is the people in this country's fault, but the people in this country haven't been informed either. I put the major part of the blame, the most guilty single party is the irresponsibility of the television medium to present the situation to us. They just give us a bunch of junk programming—they didn't spend nearly enough time to go into depth enough on the issues they confronted and they fail to do so today. They've been giving us bread and suckers when they should have been telling us what was happening."[6]

～

Despite his criticism, Turner conceded that most television journalists were trying to do a good job:

"I think that the whole news profession is full of honest people who put their careers above remunerative rewards, who are basically very idealistic and I feel that I am, too."[7]

～

Nevertheless, Turner was determined to improve the industry:

"I'm going to do the news like the world has never seen news before, this will be the most significant achievement in the annals of journalism."[8]

Turner claimed that his satellite and cable broadcasting services would be "a positive force for good": "I intend to conquer the world, but instead of conquering with bombs I intend to conquer with good ideas."[9]

~

Turner first assembled an energetic and adventurous news production team, then devoted much of his time developing the business side of CNN. While he kept track of what was happening, by delegating news authority to journalists he was able to put together a new channel in one year:

"He does not have time for it, and he knows that is where he would be most vulnerable to his detractors," said Robert Wussler, a former president of CBS-TV and one of three top managers who organized CNN. Wussler later became head of U.S. Digital Communications.[10]

~

Turner was often absent in CNN's first few years, spending weeks at a time in sailing races and preparing for his next America's Cup challenge. During this time he and his crew participated in the ill-fated 1979 British Isles Fastnet race. In the midst of key negotiations on CNN, one Turner executive looked up at the television, which was describing the northern Atlantic storm that killed 23 sailors and damaged or destroyed nearly four dozen boats. There was an interval of shock, bewilderment, and confusion when it seemed that Turner too may have perished. Happily, a few hours later Turner sailed safely and victoriously into the harbor at Cowes, England.

~

Turner and his executives worked against a nearly impossible deadline, with a budget that was a fraction of what the networks spent, and then faced a major obstacle when Satcom III, the satellite on which they had booked CNN's transmission, disappeared somewhere into the sky shortly after launch. The satellite was never recovered, and all the cable companies clamored for scarce alternate space on Satcom I. Turner had to slug it out for one of the two available transponders.

~

When CNN went on the air as scheduled, Turner said the network's role would be

> *"To create a positive force in a world where cynics abound, to provide information to people when it wasn't available before."*[11]

~

Despite his good intentions, Turner was unfamiliar with journalism and television news, and made several missteps in the beginning.

> *"We're going to do a bunch of investigative exposés on the television business. Listen, I'm going after the networks. I'm going to scare the hell out of them."*[12]

His staff soon persuaded Turner to abandon some practices that they felt were unfair and inappropriate, including the notion of doing negative stories about competitors.

~

Against producers' wishes, Turner broadcast several on-air editorials, one protesting the showing on TV of violent movies such as *The Warriors* and *Taxi Driver*, the film that sparked John Hinckley's attempted assassination of President Reagan. In that editorial, Turner insisted:

> *"The people responsible for this movie should be just as much on trial as John Hinckley himself . . . write your congressman and your senator right away, and tell him that you want something done."*[13]

~

Turner hired a *Playboy* cover girl, with whom he reportedly was having an affair, as host of a news show. Not surprisingly, the show did not work out.

~

After former CNN business editor Lou Dobbs had a heart-to-heart talk with Turner about journalism standards, Ted came to realize that he couldn't have a completely free rein with television programming. Dobbs thought he might be fired after the frank discussion with his boss, but Turner respected the newsman for his action. Dobbs stayed with CNN until 1999. Over the years, said Turner, he had to give ground on some of his early notions:

> *"You know, sometimes you have to compromise in television. I've had to do stuff and put on programs or films I didn't agree with and was not sympathetic to—though they were never as violent as some of Rupert Murdoch's shows."*[14]

~

It surely was cold comfort to Turner that CNN's highest ratings have been wrought from the coverage of violent events such as the Mount Saint Helens eruption and the O.J. Simpson murder trial.

~

At first CNN was called "chicken noodle news," but media critics knew that CNN had achieved its full wings when it covered the student uprising in China; others think CNN came of age with its coverage of the Gulf War. But newspapers and other television stations acknowledged CNN as an immutable force in 1989, when the Loma Prieta earthquake struck the San Francisco Bay area. CNN reporters with minicams covered the disaster live, moment by moment in the dramatic aftermath of the temblor. Television newscasters knew they had to provide live coverage as well. Newspaper editors were in even deeper trouble as they realized that even the best writing could never compete with watching the action as it occurred.

It took CNN several years to become a financial success. In 1980, when his network was deeply in the red, Turner put on a brave face:

"It doesn't bother me that I'm committing almost all I have. Had I known I was going to fail when I started, I would still have done it because it needs to be done. . . . Of course, I also think we'll make a fortune."[15]

Nearly a decade after CNN was founded, Turner felt that there was more work to be done and plenty of potential for growth:

"Our horizon is limitless. Our ambition is limitless. Before this year is out, we will be broadcasting CNN to the entire world. Anyone with a satellite dish anywhere in the world can watch CNN."[16]

By 1999 CNN had 36 news bureaus, 24 of them outside the United States. The network reached 80 million households.

When CNN first went on the air, Turner promised to continue broadcasting as long as possible. He played a tape of the traditional Christian hymn, "Nearer My God To Thee":

"In the event the end of the world comes, we'll play that, then sign off."

RIDE THE LEADING EDGE

In the early days of CNN, when Turner was heavily in debt and a number of competitors were betting that the network would fail, Turner was asked if he was nervous:

"Sure, I'm worried. But I'm not that worried. As soon as I earn me my billion dollars, I am going to buy a network. I am going to find the new Frank Capra and set him making movies. I can quit whenever I want to. I am not worried about what people think. But I am the right man in the right place at the right time, not me alone, but all the people who think the world can be brought together by telecommunications."[17]

~

As the years passed, Turner's television operations have remained at the cutting edge of technology, quickly embracing computers and systems based entirely on digital technology. But Turner also has continued to be a bold programmer:

He introduced his 1994 documentary, *The Native Americans*, with a speech to an audience that included an Indian dance troupe hired to entertain reporters after the press conference.

"I understand these Indians who are performing tonight are very peaceful. I mean, I don't want them scalping any of our critics here."[18]

Overall, the reviewers praised the documentary. They also smiled on Jane Fonda's companion movie, *Lakota Woman*.

Turner explained why he sponsored the making of *The Native Americans*:

> *"I'm always interested in exploring subjects that haven't really been covered. Nobody's ever taken a really in-depth look at our indigenous people. I've also always pulled for the underdog. And ever since Columbus landed, Native Americans have been the underdog."*[19]

Tom Perkins, a member of the Echota Cherokee tribe of Alabama and the owner of the Oglewanagi Gallery-American Indian Center in Atlanta, was among the indigenous Americans who criticized Turner for continuing to call his baseball team the Braves and using a fictional Indian chief as its mascot while at the same time producing a documentary on the plight of Perkins's people:

"Evidently, Ted Turner must be an extremely complex individual," Perkins said, "to be that sensitive on the one hand, yet at the same time be so insensitive to the modern-day reality that American Indians are the only race of people still being used as mascots . . . like we're lions and tigers and bears."[20]

NOTE: Turner no longer uses the term "Tomahawk chop" when cheering for the Braves. Instead, he uses the "palmahawk" wave, a native peace gesture.

CNN Interactive and the software maker Oracle introduced a new joint website called The Custom News Website at the 1997 Spring Comdex computer show. Oracle provides technology for the site, and CNN Interactive supplies the news content.

Turner claimed that simpler access to the news could be beneficial to humankind who suffer from overexposure to news. He cited a study that indicated that one-third of Americans suffered health problems brought on by the overwhelming amount of information confronting us at home and at work and during the commute between the two:

"It's affecting our love lives, for Christ's sake."[21]

⁓

"I have a computer on my desk with the stocks that I follow. I watch it go up 1/8, then down 1/8. I lose $20 million, I gain $20 million. By noon, I don't know whether I should buy lunch myself or let someone else pick up the tab. Then I watch CNN all day for all those [convicted Oklahoma City bomber Timothy] McVeigh updates . . . I have 15 TVs in my office. Then there's all the sports. This [kind of information overload] is what this customized news program is supposed to combat."[22]

⁓

Larry Ellison, Oracle's chief executive, joined Turner in explaining how CNET News.com would work. Ellison and Turner demonstrated the new web page to the bemused crowd. At first, the website wouldn't come up, then Ellison couldn't find his glasses. When Ellison finally gained access to his own customized news page, it included a breaking story about the network computer, Japan, and the Olympics. It also showed updates of his chosen stocks, Oracle, Netscape, and Microsoft.

But then Ellison had difficulty customizing a news page for Turner. After some tinkering, the score of the previous night's Braves game showed up—San Diego Padres 5, Atlanta Braves 2.

Turner burst out, "That sure took a long time. I knew that last night."[23]

A SPORTS EMPIRE

THROWING HEAT

Ted Turner bought the Atlanta Braves from the Atlanta-LaSalle Corporation in January 1976 and thus began a soap opera episode, both in Turner's life and the lives of Atlanta sports fans. The Braves, sad to say, were holding up last place in the National League West.

How did Ted Turner come to buy the Braves?

"Purely by accident. We were televising their games, and, as the rights holder, I got pretty close to management. So, when they decided to sell the team, they approached me as the logical buyer. The thought had never occurred to me."[1]

It wasn't because Turner was a lifelong baseball fan. A small boy for his age, who didn't handle balls well, Turner didn't play much baseball as a kid. But once he got interested in the Atlanta Braves, he became an avid fan.

Turner, of course, was no stranger to buying distressed properties. When he realized that the owners, discouraged at the Braves' losing streak, were going to sell the team and allow it to move out of town, Turner stepped in. The Braves were an important part of WTBG's programming. Not only would the sale leave a big hole in the Superstation's week, but viewers from around the United States who had become Braves fans by watching the cable broadcast of games might switch stations.

Turner purchased the Braves for $11 million, agreeing to a $1 million down payment. The remainder was to be paid out of revenues over the years. Immediately after acquiring the team, Turner discovered $1 million in a bank account from stadium concessions that the former owners didn't know existed. Basically, he bought the team with no money down.[2]

~

Phyllis Collins, a secretary for the Braves management, attended Turner's first meeting with the team: "He said he wasn't going to make us any promises. He said when he got married the first time he made a lot of promises he didn't live up to and his wife got mad at him. In his second marriage he made no promises, and now he gets applause when he comes through. That's the way it would be with the Braves."[3]

No promises, but Turner did make changes, moving the start of the business day from 9 A.M. to 8:30.

He also shook up the baseball establishment by doing things owners weren't supposed to do.

⁓

Although the Turner family has a private box, when Ted used to attend games regularly, he sat behind the first-base dugout, shouting at coaches, players, and umpires like any other fan might do.

> *"I never could understand why owners like to sit up behind bulletproof glass sipping martinis. I sit in the front row."*[4]

⁓

Turner hoped to establish friendly relations with the players, to create a familylike atmosphere in the Braves clubhouse. His attitude regarding player grooming—a big issue in the 1970s—was liberal:

> *"Hell, you've got a beard and I've got a mustache. I don't care what a ballplayer does, if it makes him happy, it makes me happy. Just as long as he wears something over his cock, you know."*[5]

⁓

Turner did hope the team would start playing better:

> *"I don't want to see any more 'Loserville' headlines in the Atlanta papers."*[6]

⁓

To draw crowds to the baseball park, Turner brought in sideshow entertainment. Ted himself participated in such gimmicks as the Great Mattress Stacking Championship, pushing a baseball around the field using his nose, and a race around the field's perimeter in surreys pulled by ostriches. It was madness with a purpose:

> *"When you're little, you have to do crazy things. You just can't copy the big guys. To succeed you have to be innovative."*[7]

~

Phil Niekro, the Braves' pitcher, felt Turner enjoyed being on the field. "He enjoys it more than anyone in the ball park. He'd really like to put on a uniform and play in the game. He ran with us and worked out in spring training. He communicates with the players, and I know his enthusiasm rubbed off on us. I think he'll have the same effect on the fans," Niekro explained.[8]

~

> *"I'm the little guy's hero. They love me. I run the team the way they think they would if they owned it. I come to all the games. Sit in the stands. Drink a few beers. Even take my shirt off. I'm Mr. Everyman to them—their pal, Ted."*[9]

~

Asked if he was living out the little boy's dream of owning a baseball team, Turner replied: "Sort of. But you know what I do dig? Being a folk hero. Because I am just one of the folk."[10]

~

Baseball commissioner Bowie Kuhn didn't necessarily agree that Turner was the sport's new hero. He didn't think it was ownerly when Turner ran out on the field to welcome a slugger to home base, or played poker or traveled with team members.

DON'T TOUCH THE GRASS

Visitors to Turner Field in Atlanta can take a tour of the former Olympic stadium and the grounds, but when they walk toward the playing field, the guide politely requests, "Please don't touch the grass." The field's turf is costly, supplied from the Florida farm of golfer Greg Norman. It is carefully groomed to make it ideal for baseball and an emerald perfection to the eyes of the television cameras.

Commissioner Kuhn didn't have handsome turf in mind when he ordered Ted Turner to get off the field—in fact, told him leave the ballpark altogether and stay away for a full year.

Turner first got under Kuhn's skin when, on April 10, 1976, he cracked open baseball's free agent situation by hiring pitcher Andy Messersmith with a $1 million, three-year package.

Several years later Turner conceded that he had made a mistake with the Messersmith deal:

"I'm through with this free agent stuff. I was a rookie owner and I made some mistakes. I tell you,

I've gone to the well for the last time. Hey, people aren't supposed to beat on a rookie."[11]

~

Turner further irritated other baseball owners and Kuhn by offering a $500 bonus to his players for every game over 81 that they won and an additional 5 percent over their salaries for every 100,000 paid admissions over 900,000 at the end of the season. Ever the advertising man, Turner was offering sales incentives to the team members.[12]

~

Turner got seriously crosswise with Kuhn when the Braves offered left-fielder Gary Matthews a five-year, $1.5 million contract. Turner had first approached Matthews casually at a cocktail party, which by league rules was forbidden. Kuhn decided Turner had to be punished.

Turner knew what was coming and sized up the prospects this way:

"Well, there are a couple of things he could do. First of all, he could return Gary Matthews to the Giants. But that wouldn't be punishing me. That would be punishing him. Or he could fine me a lot of money. But I've got a lot of money. If he fines me a lot of money, he knows I'll pay it and then I'll go on my merry way. Or he could really *punish me, and at the same time get me out of his hair, by suspending me from baseball. When we go to the winter [league]*

meetings, we've got to make sure he suspends me from baseball."[13]

~

When the Los Angeles league meeting rolled around, Turner made certain that attention shifted away from Matthews and to himself. At the Los Angeles Hilton, Turner began ranting to a crowd in the lobby: "The commissioner of baseball is going to kill me! Bowie Kuhn is out to kill me. My life is over."[14]

~

Turner kept the pressure up when he met with Kuhn and implored: "Great White Father, I am very contrite. I am very humble. I am sorry. I would get down on the floor and let you jump up and down on me if it would help. I would let you hit me three times in the face without lifting a hand to protect myself. I would bend over and let you paddle my behind, hit me over the head with a Fresca bottle."[15]

~

When Kuhn suspended Turner from baseball, more than 40,000 Atlantans signed a petition on his behalf, but to no avail.

~

Turner may have been throwing heat, but his pitchers were not. Ted felt that his team was playing so badly that he could manage the Braves as well as anyone else. He realized his dream—briefly—for one game on May 11, 1977. The Braves were still in their losing streak, and Kuhn had temporarily lifted Turner's suspension. Turner took over management of the team but lost the game anyway, making it the seventeenth straight loss. Kuhn promptly cabled Turner and told him to cut it out, because he didn't have the necessary baseball management experience. Turner phoned Kuhn and asked how else he was going to get the experience.

"In the stands, like other owners. Why can't you be like everybody else?"

"Because," retorted Turner, "my team is in last place."[16]

～

"The trouble with me is I say what I think. That's really why Kuhn suspended me."[17]

～

Turner took his suspension philosophically:

"The world has gotten along without Abraham Lincoln, John Kennedy, and Jesus Christ. Baseball can get along without me...."[18]

And of course Turner had other things to do that summer than sit in a baseball park. He immediately packed off to Rhode Island and won the 1977 America's Cup yachting race.

～

NOTE: Again, Turner took a risky position but got poor results. Several years later, when Matthews wasn't playing well, Turner and the Braves manager forced the outfielder off the team.

◠

In 1980, for a second time, Ted Turner was investigated by Commissioner Kuhn for alleged tampering with free agent Dave Winfield by inviting him to an extravagant Halloween party. Turner was cleared of those charges.[19]

The worm turned several years later when Turner was in the position of helping to eject Kuhn from baseball.

Many owners voted against renewing Kuhn's contract in 1982, including Turner. Philadelphia Phillies president Bill Giles had an interesting perspective on the meeting at which Kuhn's fate was decided. "Ted Turner listed eight reasons why he would not vote to renew Kuhn's term," said Giles. "He was the only one that I thought had legitimate reasons. He presented his case well; he was not vindictive. The other National League people just didn't give decent reasons why you should not vote for him."[20]

◠

Asked about his 1982 team-owner vote against the baseball commissioner's contract, Turner said: "Bowie has been in office almost 14 years, and is baseball better off than it was 14 years ago? No, it is not. Certainly it is not better off financially. Whose fault is that? It may not be Bowie Kuhn's fault, but he's the leader. It's not always the manager's fault either [when a team plays badly], but he's the guy you fire—right?"[21]

~

What might make Turner change his vote in favor of Kuhn?

"Maybe I'll call him and say, 'I'll make a deal with you. If you let me manage, I'll change my vote.' That's how they get bills passed in Congress, you know. Making deals. But I'm only kidding about changing my vote. Only kidding."[22]

HOME OF THE BRAVES

A massive American flag whips in the wind above Turner Field in Atlanta, and a billboard proclaims the arena to be the Home of the Braves. With the team's playing history, it has sometimes required courage to be an Atlanta Braves fan.

When he first bought the team, Turner fought valiantly to improve the Braves' league standing. When the Braves finished last in the National League West for the fourth season, Turner became more philosophical:

"I look at baseball as kind of my little extra burden that I have. Some people have to live with diabetes. I

have to live with a losing baseball team . . . better a losing team than none at all."23

~

"It's good for my humility. As my father used to say, 'A few fleas on a dog help remind him of what he is.'"24

~

In the early 1980s, Turner admitted that the team was draining off a lot of money:

"With the Braves, the losses are massive. Like you don't mind giving a pint of blood to the Red Cross once in a while, but to give a gallon every day, you're going to be bled white and it's not so much fun. But it's not the end of the world. I'd rather have my country be free and have a last place club than a first-place club and a communist country."25

~

In 1978 a *Playboy* interviewer asked Turner why he continued to be so optimistic about the future of such a dismal team:

Turner: "Why do you think my own racing yacht is named *Tenacious*, dummy?"

Playboy: "We give up. Why?"

Turner: "Because I never quit. I've got a bunch of flags on my boat, but there ain't no white flags. I don't surrender. That's the story of my life. Just think, if you were a rabbit, to survive, you'd have to hop fast and keep your eyes open. 'Ride, boldly ride,' the shade replied—'if you seek for Eldorado.'"[26]

～

By 1981 Turner was becoming increasingly sanguine:

"This is a sport we're talking about here. Not a war, but a sport. It's not like we're talking about MX missiles or B-1 bombers. We're talking about balls and strikes. I'd like to win, but I'd rather see inflation under control or see people stop shooting the Pope and Sadat. Baseball is a business, but it's still a game. And I like to keep it in perspective."[27]

～

In 1982 Turner tried to persuade baseball star Reggie Jackson to join the Braves.

"I did everything I could, but I suspect Reggie is going to sign with the Yankees. It's okay. It's not that disappointing to me. If we didn't have Brett Butler and Ed Miller, it would be a lot more disappointing.

"Oh well. Reggie and I still are buddies. We'll always be buddies, just like Pete Rose and I will always be buddies, just like Tommy Lasorda and I will always be buddies. But you don't get somebody to play for you just because he is your buddy."[28]

～

Despite the the failure to lure Jackson to the team, Turner predicted that the Atlanta Braves would win the pennant that year. Asked why he felt so sure, Turner replied: "Lots of reasons, including the fact we don't have any crazies, flakes, or drug addicts on the team."[29]

~

At last, the Turner magic started working and the season went well:

> *"I'm very, very pleased with what's been happening down here. Ecstatic. Enthusiastic. Tickled pink. We're going to finish first, and I just wish Bill Lucas [the late general manager] were alive to see it. Atlanta will go berserk. I'm getting ready to hoist the pennant because we're going to win one. How do you hoist a pennant anyway? Like this?"[30]*

~

Turner's Braves finally won the National League West championship in 1982 after six losing years. Turner was beside himself:

> *"A few years ago, people were asking me how it felt to lose 100 games in a season. Now ask me how it feels to be a champion. It feels great. It's wonderful. How do you think it feels? . . . Of all the things I have done in my life, nothing has made me happier than this."[31]*

~

Team member Jerry Royster expressed his personal relief. "The past seven years have been rough. We've been through 100-loss seasons, through 17-game losing streaks, through total embarrassment," said Royster. "It's been unreal, one bad thing after another, and now we finally get this . . . Everything else Ted Turner has ever been involved in, except us, has been a success. I'm just glad we're a success now, too."[32]

~

The Atlanta Braves have since played in four World Series, 1991, 1992, 1995, and 1996. The team won the Series in 1995, the first World Series victory for the Braves in 38 years and the first win since the team called Atlanta home. The Braves are the only team to have won the series in three cities. They took the championship in 1914 while playing in Boston and again in 1957 when they were based in Milwaukee. In 1994 the National League was reorganized and the Braves were reassigned to the National League East. In 1998 the team won its seventh straight division title.

~

The Atlanta Braves now pack Turner Field for most games. Time Warner renamed the former Olympic Stadium in Atlanta after Turner, angering some Georgians who favored giving the honor to baseball legend and Atlanta businessman Hank Aaron.

~

The stadium was the venue for track and field and other outdoor events during the 1996 summer Olympics. It took seven months for the Braves' management to transform the space into one of the finest small baseball fields in America.

Game-night entertainment remains lively and family oriented. At a June 1999 game between the Braves and the Baltimore Orioles, an 11-year-old girl read the team lineups; a 10-year-old girl sang a sparkling rendition of the "Star Spangled Banner" while a 12-year-old boy stood beside her and translated the words into sign language; all the city's Little League teams paraded around the field in a pregame ceremony, and awards were handed out to the top players. Braves batters stepped up to the plate to their own snappy theme songs, and members of the audience made trip after trip to Turner Field's food court for sodas, beer, and foot-long hot dogs. Families with children were invited to hang out in a playroom called "Tooner Field," where Hanna-Barbera cartoons rolled across television monitors around the room. Nearly 20 years after Turner bought the team, an Atlanta Braves game is more than baseball. It is a big night out, even if the Braves do lose to the Baltimore Orioles 22 to 1.

∼

Turner finally gave up on building a familylike team. Not only did Turner learn that other team owners were hostile to his style, he realized that camaraderie carried no weight when negotiating player contracts. Gradually Turner began acting more like other owners.

In 1986 Bucky Woy, agent for baseball hitter Bob Horner, said of Turner, "If you aren't prepared, he'll smell blood and go for the kill. He'll bury you."[33]

~

When Turner ordered Horner down to the minor leagues, he was heavily criticized in the Atlanta press. Soon afterward Turner was interviewed by *Sport* magazine and asked if he loved sports, since he then owned two professional sports teams. Turner said he did not love baseball; in fact he was disgusted with it. "This whole incident [Horner] has made me think seriously about getting out of it completely. I bore the four years of last place with equanimity and grace. I bore my suspension and all the other things . . . I mean, to me baseball is just a silly little game, like croquet or anything else that happens to be popular."[34]

~

Later in the interview the reporter asked Turner another question about Horner's demotion:

> *"I'm tired of talking about Bob Horner. There are very few 22-year-old players that call the owner a jerk after he just gave them a million-dollar contract. The next time you ask me about Horner, this interview's over."*[35]

When the reporter asked if Horner's return to a Braves' uniform without going to the minors was a victory for the player, Turner declared the interview over.

~

Turner continues to remind people to keep sports in a sane perspective:

> *"Sports mean fun and games. They're diversion. Sports are something you do in your spare time. I mean only a very wealthy society like ours could afford all this emphasis on professional athletes who don't have any other job than to play a few games."*[36]

THE HAWKS AND OTHER TEAMS

> *"Nobody in the history of the world has lost as much money in sports as I have. It's reached the point where I judge my success by how big a loss I can absorb."*[37]

~

Turner's teams might have been considered unprofitable when evaluated as stand-alone propositions, but his television stations have benefited from many hours of cheap athletics programming. For example, in 1988 Turner bought the privately held National Wrestling Alliance for about $8 million and renamed it World Championship Wrestling. The WCW, with bouts starring wrestlers like Lex Lugar and "Nature Boy" Rick Flair, is a distant second to the World Wrestling Federation, whose wrestlers include the much-adored Hulk Hogan. Even so, the WCW provided four hours a week of popular air-time entertainment for Turner's Superstation.[38]

~

In addition to the Atlanta Braves and the WCW, Turner Broadcasting System, now a subsidiary of Time Warner Inc., owns the Hawks, a National Basketball Association team, and the Thrashers, a hockey team. The Thrashers started playing in the 1999–2000 season in the new $250 million, 18,500-seat Omni Arena. Through Time Warner, Turner owns all of Atlanta's major sports teams except the Falcons, a National Football League team. There are recurring rumors that Turner will buy the Falcons as well.

~

In Turner's early years the Braves had a mascot called "The Bleacher Creature," which was made complete with a small fuzzy toy parents could buy for their children or other childlike fans. Chief Nocahoma, to whom Native Americans objected, has also been a popular symbol for the Braves. By 1999 the mascots were Hanna Barbera characters from the Cartoon Channel—Fred Flintstone and Yogi Bear.

There is a circular relationship between most all of Turner's enterprises. They feed off of and promote one another. When visitors complete a tour of the CNN Center in Atlanta, they are dropped off at the door of the CNN gift shop. But just across the way they can also buy Atlanta Braves memorabilia. At Atlanta Braves games, fans are subjected to scoreboard advertisements for CNN, ESPN, the Superstation,

Thrasher hockey tickets, and other Time Warner stuff, not to mention Turner's own buffalo steaks.

Turner once compared TBS operations to chicken farming:

> *"Modern chicken farmers, they grind up the feet to make fertilizer, they grind up the intestines to make dog food. The feathers go into pillows. Even the chicken manure they make into fertilizer. They use every bit of the chicken. Well, that's what we try to do over here with the television products, is use everything to its fullest extent."[39]*

~

Atlanta lawyer John M. Kelly lifted a beer in a toast to Turner and said, "I love the guy for what he has done for sports in Atlanta."

Just before downing the beer Kelly added, "I just hope I don't ever have to meet the s.o.b."[40]

THE GOODWILL GAMES

In the early 1980s Turner decided he needed to understand better what was happening in the world. He began a world odyssey to visit other nations and their leaders. As a result of his travels and discussions, he became disturbed about Cold War boycotts of the Olympic Games in 1980 and again in 1984. He felt that the exclusion of athletes from any country was a violation of the Olympic spirit and a detriment to the quest for world peace and universal brotherhood.

Turner came up with the idea of holding his own event—the Goodwill Games.

> *"I thought, how can we go back and undo the wrongs that occurred both ways and start all over again? I thought, with the danger of the continuation of the nuclear arms race and the threat to all the people on the planet, how nice it would be to start over again. And I thought if I could do anything to bring the sides back together on the athletic fields, it'd lessen the chances of nuclear war."*[41]

~

> *"We can best achieve peace by letting the peoples of the world get to know each other better. Not only will the participants compete together in the spirit of good sportsmanship, but the audiences worldwide will see the harmony that can be fostered among nations."*[42]

~

The first Goodwill Games, envisioned by Ted Turner and organized by his staff, were played July 5 through 20, 1986, in Moscow. Goodwill Games athletes competed in 18 sports, ranging from track and field, to tennis, to judo, to yachting.[43]

The Games were plagued with problems that year. Some key athletes would not attend and audiences were small. Critics charged that the games were not motivated by Turner's interest in world brotherhood but rather by the need to provide competitive programming for CNN, which did not have rights to broadcast the Olympics.

~

Despite the difficulties, Turner seemed happy with the games:

"I'm so happy with the way things are going. I'm having a hard time keeping from jumping out of my skin."[44]

It was apparent those initial Goodwill Games would be a financial failure, but Turner refused to cut costs, saying he wanted the games to be a first-class event. When the final tab was in, Turner lost $26 million.[45]

~

The media was a little puzzled with Turner, who flew with his own large entourage to watch the games. The group reportedly included his wife, five children, two girlfriends, and 75 of his friends from the cable television industry.[46]

~

The second Goodwill Games were held in Seattle, Washington, in July 1990. On that event, Turner lost $44 million. But the games themselves were a success, and plans began for the 1994 event.

The criticism persists that the Goodwill Games are a CNN entertainment ploy, but Turner insisted that he is not trying to preempt the Olympics. He made financial contributions to the Atlanta Olympics and held no ill feelings about the broadcast rights:

"NBC has said there will be no cable package [in 1996]. That's out. I haven't complained once. Our relationship with the Olympic Games is on a high level."[47]

~

Subsequent Goodwill Games were played in St. Petersburg, Russia, in 1994 and New York City in 1998. The usual four-year rotation of the games has been changed so as not to conflict with the 2002 Winter Olympics and the World Cup Soccer match. Instead, the games will be held in Brisbane, Australia, in September and October 2001. In the meantime, the first Winter Goodwill Games will be staged at Lake Placid, New York, in late February 2000. The prime-time Goodwill Games events will be broadcast on the TBS Superstation and on Turner Network Television (TNT).

THE NEXT BIG THING

CHALLENGE UP

Ted Turner claims that if you take on large targets, you move up to their ranks:

> *"If there's a big guy and a little guy in an argument, if the big guy will argue with him, the big guy doesn't come down to his level. The little guy rises up to his level. . . . Think of Jesus Christ. Jesus Christ was just an itinerant little preacher until the Roman Empire decided it was gonna attack him. . . . And look where he ended up."*[1]

～

Bob Hope, not the comedian but the Braves' longtime publicist, said Turner had a Don Quixote attitude: "His theory is that you don't get rolling until the big guy gets on you," said Hope. "Keep the attack upward, have a fierce dog fight with the people above you, and you rise to their level. Turner figures none of us put out until we are challenged."[2]

～

Once CNN was organized, running, and recognized as a success, Turner then aspired to buy one of the big three television networks, ABC, CBS, or NBC:

"You know if we could get our hands on one of the three major networks, which is one of the things I want to do, make an acquisition of one of them and blow the other two out of the water just the way we blew Satellite News Channels out of the water.

"I've said that before. Someday, though, I'm going to do it, but don't go out and buy the networks stocks because whichever one I get, I would make the other two virtually bankrupt. That's because I could operate so much more efficiently than the others. The networks are dinosaurs."[3]

~

"We were losing clout with advertisers to the networks, I told myself, 'Turner, if you don't do something you won't make it!' I saw that to get ahead, we either had to dominate programming or distribution. I went after the network for its distribution."[4]

~

In 1985 Turner tried a hostile takeover bid for CBS, using a lot of junk bonds and a little cash. The effort failed and cost him $21 million. Despite the frustration and cost of the effort, Turner continued to look for ways to grow the company:

"We don't really have to have a [broadcast] network. But we want to be bigger. We're trying to keep up

with the Joneses—and the Murdochs and the Red-stones and the Buffetts."[5]

~

"I want to be able to stand at the first-class table, I don't want people pushing me around anymore."[6]

~

Terence McGuirk, who in 1995 was Turner's operations chief at Turner Broadcasting System, explained, "Mr. Turner's mandate to be 'the biggest and the best entertainment company in the world' hasn't changed. And we're not going to get there growing internally. There has to be external growth."[7]

~

As if there were ever any doubt, Turner declared: "The game I'm in is building assets."[8]

THE WORST OF DEALS, THE BEST OF DEALS

Turner was in a funk when he could not buy the CBS television network, but shortly after he gave up trying, Ted received a telephone call from Las Vegas billionaire dealmaker Kirk Kerkorian. Kerkorian offered Turner the opportunity to acquire his movie studio, Metro-Goldwyn-Mayer/United Artists.

The offer intrigued Turner, but during his negotiations, it became known that Mohamed Al Fayed (whose son later died in the Paris automobile accident with Princess Diana) also was interested in buying the studio. Turner hates to haggle and quickly accepted Kerkorian's asking price of $1.6 billion, roughly double the $826 million market value of MGM/UA.

Turner admitted freely: "I didn't negotiate on price."[9]

~

By accepting Kirk Kerkorian's figure, Turner became hot gossip in both the TV industry and on Wall Street. It made Turner look worse when, near the end of the negotiations to finance the deal, Drexel Burnham junk bond financier Michael Milken arbitrarily upped his fees from $80 million to $140 million.

One analyst observed, "It's one of the nuttiest deals of all time." Another said, "Ted Turner came to town fully clothed and left in a barrel."[10]

~

After the MGM/UA contract was signed, Turner learned that some of the movies he bought to show on his television channels were already spoken for. Some Time Inc. officials told him casually, "Well, Ted, you know we've leased a number of those films, they're locked up."

> *"Goddam it!"* Ted shouted. *"I've never done anything like this before. It's like sailboat racing in a hurricane. It's like being in an airplane in a storm. You buckle your seat belt."[11]*

~

Perhaps in a state of nervous agitation, Turner boasted of his debt burden to his mother: "Two billion dollars I owe! Actually it's closer to one point nine, but I like the sound of two billion better."

"Oh my," said his mother. "How much did he say?"

"*Two billion*," shouted Ted. "No individual in history has ever owed more."

"Oh Ted, I get a headache thinking about it. Well you're honest, you'll try and pay it all back, I know," declared his mother.

"That's a million dollars a day in interest, Mother. Here, look at my picture in today's newspaper. Do I look worried?"[12]

~

What happened next bore an eerie resemblance to the situation Ed Turner believed he was in shortly before he committed suicide. It became obvious that Ted could not meet the $2 billion debt load.

"At the time the MGM deal was a mistake. I mean, if you say, 'I just made a deal that requires me to give away half my company,' when that wasn't the intent of the deal—well, it might work out in the future, but at the time it clearly was a miscalculation."[13]

~

"Assuming things don't work out the way I've planned, I'm going to do what I've always done, I've been running this company for 23 years and virtually

107

every one of those years someone predicted I was either going to lose control, or sell out, or go broke.

"Business is tough right now, but listen: For me, business has always been tough. I grew up in a tough neighborhood. We pioneered everything we started— we pioneered ad-supported cable, we pioneered 24-hour news, we pioneered global networks. We've had to fight and scrap every inch of the way against entrenched powerful competitors. We've survived and none of our competitors have. They're there, but they've all changed hands and are in different forms."[14]

∿

"Ted has been on the edge financially with MGM," Time Inc. executive Nick Nicholas observed, "but I wouldn't bet against him. Maybe he wins so much because he knows where the edge is."[15]

∿

To free himself from the tight spot, Turner sold the film studio, the cassette business, and the MGM logo rights back to Kerkorian for a lot less money than he had paid. He retained the 3,600 films that he wanted so badly. Turner was able to reduce his debt, although he was still more than a billion dollars in the red. However, if Turner still wasn't able to make his payments, Kerkorian had the right to foreclose.

∿

Turner said he realized that he'd bet the family store on a risky proposition: ". . . There are some risks involved with it, of course, but there are risks involved with everything. Even to get here [for the reporter's interview] you've risked a lot. Life is a series of gambles, and you know the final outcome is going to be a tragic one. So since you're dead—the day you're born, you start to die—you have to be willing to accept risks in business, and there have been risks all along. I think we're in a less risky position today than we've ever been."[16]

～

"If a major recession caught me in a high debt cycle, I'd be in trouble. But so would Chase Manhattan and a lot of others. I think my wife would stick with me. My dog would still love me. If I could afford birdseed, my cockatoo would stick around. A lot of friends wouldn't."[17]

～

Turner had a chance to find out. He got into hot water a second time when he couldn't come up with the hundreds of millions of dollars of payments owed Kerkorian.

～

In June 1986 Turner and some of his cable industry colleagues, including John Malone, Nick Nicholas, and Michael Fuchs, took a tour of the MGM studios, after which they met to discuss how to save Ted's empire and make the MGM purchase work. While these executives talked, Turner busily scribbled numbers on the back of an envelope, trying to figure a way he could retain the studio. One executive recalls, "I was thinking about the way our company would do it—9 million accountants, 10,000 lawyers. Here was Ted, doing this deal on the back of an envelope."[18]

~

This time Turner was forced to sell 37 percent of his company for $562.5 million to a consortium of cable companies led by TCI chairman John Malone. The cable operators knew that CNN and Turner's products were so important to their cable programming that they could neither allow the company to fail nor let it fall into the hands of someone with a different vision from Turner's.[19]

~

Malone saw it this way: "If we hadn't rescued Ted Turner, TBS would have been bought by Rupert Murdoch, and CNN now would be running Murder of the Week."[20]

~

"We felt that a financially healthy TBS was vital to our future," said Tim Neher, president of Boston's Continental Cablevision. "If we didn't rescue Turner, someone else would, and they might not share our interests in continuing the same quality of programs. Why turn CNN over to a broadcaster who would distribute it over the air?"[21]

~

Turner realized that despite his debt, his role in the cable industry gave him some power over the situation:

"We're going to win together or lose together. Nobody wins if you get into a war."[22]

~

In exchange for providing Turner with the half a billion dollars to pay off Kerkorian, the cable operators received more than one-third of the company's equity and 16 percent of its voting stock. Turner retained 51 percent of the equity and 67.8 percent of the voting stock. The cable operators didn't like his "one-man band" management style, but Turner remained as the head of the company. He was the only member of the board who owed so much money that he was no threat to the others.

Although Turner still owned a majority interest in the company and kept his title, the restructuring agreement called for him to answer to a powerful board. In many ways it turned out to be a good committee, including such proven executives as Malone, Michael Fuchs of HBO, Gerald Levin of Time Warner, and others.

~

Convincing a committee to go along with his ideas had not been Turner's style, but when he talked to a reporter from *Broadcasting* magazine, Ted seemed ready to give it a try:

Turner: "I believe that in order to solve the problems of today, we have to work together. We've got to strengthen the United Nations. We're going to have to learn to get along with everybody. And that's a big difference, that's a major change. And in order for me to be able to espouse that philosophy and promulgate it, I have to have partners of my own and learn how to get along with them."

Broadcasting: "Does that mean you have to be quieter?"

Turner: "Well, yes, I mean when you've got partners, you have to spend some time listening. You can't be talking all the time."[23]

~

The reporter asked Turner if he knew he was in trouble after the MGM acquisition:

Turner: "I knew I was in trouble before I bought MGM. That's why I bought it. I maintain we were in much more trouble before we got into it."

Broadcasting: "How much trouble?"

Turner: ". . . We did not have any proprietary programming for WTBS to speak of. We had the Braves and we had a little [Jacques] Cousteau [programming] and some of the documentaries we had done, but we were at the mercy of Hollywood. And I wanted to use our position to move to the next level, which was to own a library—and a fine library—so that we could control enough programming that we could program a really fine entertainment network, not only in the United States but globally, to position ourselves in the global business. I felt like—and still feel like—that if you just have distribution today, and that's basically what the three networks have, you're very vulnerable."[24]

~

Before long Turner began to regather his strength. His channels made such good use of the film library that MGM minority shareholders later sued the studio directors, insisting that MGM assets had been sold too cheaply. Turner felt vindicated.

"I may make a mistake someday, but buying MGM wasn't one of them."[25]

~

"We've got 35 percent of the great films of all time! We've got Spencer Tracy and Jimmy Cagney working for us from the grave!"[26]

~

While watching a colorized version of the black-and-white movie *Casablanca*, Turner crowed: "I knew it would be great. I just knew it! I'm no [dodo]. I already knew about colorization when I bought the library. I knew it would make these movies worth 10

113

times as much. Doesn't this just blow your mind? You'd never know that wasn't shot yesterday. The whole thing about colorization destroying films [referring to the appearances before Congress by, among others, Woody Allen and Steven Spielberg to denounce colorization as the pillage of a priceless cultural legacy] is just stupid. Women put on makeup every day and no one bitches about that."[27]

~

The success of Turner Classic Movies was never more evident than in the summer of 1999 when first the *New York Times* and then *The Wall Street Journal* published essays in praise of TCM. "For some time there have been signs that a large number of American are now hopelessly addicted to the Turner Classic Movies network," wrote Dorothy Rabinowitz in *The Wall Street Journal*. "So much so that they would cheerfully relinquish all else on television, and possibly their day jobs, to keep their TCM."

Rabinowitz explained, "The reasons for that dependency are perfectly clear. The TCM network, which now reaches 33 million households, can offer selections from a library of some 5,000 films from MGM, pre-1948 Warner Brothers, RKO, Columbia, Fox, and Paramount—classics, minor curiosities, great films half forgotten or never before seen, movies no one ever thought it possible to see again."[28]

To make matters even better, TCM offers its films without commercial interruption.

~

The whole MGM/UA episode represented a personal triumph for Turner. Although he was faced with problems his father could not handle, Ted showed that he learned a lot during his turbulent life. He could survive the severest storm.

~

"I showed everyone it made a lot of sense to buy MGM, I showed 'em."[29]

TIME WARNER

Although Turner's new board of directors guarded him from what they considered reckless actions, Turner eventually felt that they held the company on a short tether.

In 1989 Turner's board had vetoed his proposal to buy Financial News Network (FNN) for slightly more than $100 million. They also nixed his plans to broadcast major league baseball. In order to buy New Line Cinema and Castle Rock Entertainment, Turner said he almost had to "go to war" with other board members.[30]

One of TBS's board members, HBO chairman Fuchs said, "Ted is impulsive. Ted has one speed—full speed ahead, but the board slows decisions down at the right times. It lends a balance; that is the reason Turner Broadcasting is in terrific shape today."[31]

Ted, however, claimed: "I'm not reckless, not a gambler at all."[32]

~

Fuchs didn't fully trust Turner, and the feeling seemed mutual. Jeffrey Sonnenfeld, a management professor at Emory University, said, "Ted mentioned to me once that when he first met Michael Fuchs, he thought Fuchs had a poison tip at the end of his umbrella."[33]

~

Turner persisted in his attempts to acquire a network, insisting he had a good reason for doing so:

"Size in this business is important. It's the same with packaged goods or soft drinks. You tell me who controls shelf space at the supermarket, the No.7 brand or the No.1? People don't know the No. 7 brand exists."[34]

~

Turner found himself in competition with Time Warner (which owned 29 percent of his company) in his effort to buy the NBC television network:

"Time Warner is trying to get a network and is holding me back from doing so, and that's not right."[35]

~

In a 1994 speech at the Washington Press Club, Turner complained: "They're holding me back! I'll tell you one thing: We ran a story on clitorectomies. Most people don't know about it, but millions of women have their clitorises cut off before they are 10 or 12 years old, so they can't have fun in sex. Between 50 percent and 80 percent of Egyptian girls have had their clits cut off. You talk about barbaric mutilation. . . . Well, I'm angry. I'm being clitorized by Time Warner."[36]

∼

Turner and Time Warner chairman Gerry Levin had known each other for many years. When Turner was planning the launch of CNN in 1978, he called Levin (at what was then Time Inc.) and offered him part ownership in the project in return for a share of the investment costs. Levin declined. Again in 1983, Turner offered Time half of CNN for $350 million. Nicholas J. Nicholas, the Time executive who declined the second offer, called it the single biggest mistake of his career.[37]

∼

The competition to acquire the networks became increasingly frenzied, and Turner bemoaned the trend toward a few larger companies controlling the television and the cable business:

> *"I think all three networks will be realigned with other companies. It's an absolute tragedy that we'll end up with four or five mega-companies that will control everything that we see."[38]*

Turner predicted that Walt Disney, Viacom, and Time Warner would all acquire networks. Turner's nemesis Rupert Murdoch, whom he once called a "mad genius," already owned Fox Network.[39]

Turner lamented his lack of success:

"I'm trying hard. I call them every month. I wake up in the middle of the night sometimes gritting my teeth. . . . And I'd just beat the bed with my fist; I've got no network."[40]

"If I died tomorrow, you know what my tombstone's going to say? It'll say, 'He never got a major network.' That's what it's going to say."[41]

Turner was never able to acquire a major network, but he found an unexpected way to expand his empire. He merged Turner Broadcasting Co. with Time Warner, making TBS a subsidiary of Time Warner.

A former TBS executive said he thought that Turner realized that he couldn't get the money to buy a TV network without investors who would restrict him. "He probably looked at his smaller army and said commanding the Northern troops in this version of Ted's Civil War is a better place to be."[42]

When Turner sold TBS to Time Warner on October 10, 1995, the company became the world's largest entertainment conglomerate and Turner became a much richer man. Time Warner controls the largest concentration of cable channels in the world, including CNN, Home Box Office, the Cartoon Network, TBS, and TNT.

The total deal was valued at $8 billion; Turner got about $2.3 billion of Time Warner stock. Some compensation experts claim that Turner earned an additional $100 million through stock options and bonuses.[43] With 11 percent of Time Warner stock he is the company's largest shareholder.

"You only live once, and you ought to have all the experiences you can. I want to see what it's like to be big before I die."[44]

~

Mike Milken helped Turner raise money for his various merger plans over the years, and according to some news reports, Turner appreciated his help and advice. In the intervening years Milken was convicted of fraud and served time in prison, but by 1995 he was again involved in some financial activities. According to the reports, Turner paid Milken $50 million, $10 million out of his own pocket, the rest from TBS, for his advice during the Time Warner merger. One Wall Streeter claimed, "This is Ted's way of saying, 'You saved me in the 1980's.' Ted is bending over backward to go out of his way to give something back to Mike."[45]

~

The Time Warner merger resulted in about 1,000 lay-offs, a sweep that affected the Turner family right along with everyone else. Turner's 33-year-old son Teddy was working at the company, and at a family dinner, asked his father about his job security.

"You're toast," Ted snapped, then went on to explain. "It's good for the company, and it's good for you. In the short run it's always a little painful."

Later in the evening Turner became remorseful, agonizing to his wife, Jane, "I fired my own son."

Apparently Teddy wasn't worried. ". . . if worse comes to worse he'll get me a job."[46]

~

Turner cut 500 to 1,000 jobs at Turner Broadcasting. His eyes filled with tears when he said: "One had been with the company for 35 years. He was 60 years old, laid off. It has been so hard. It's almost as if my heart has been torn from my body. My own son got laid off. I would almost rather die than go through that again."[47]

~

A few minutes after that heartfelt statement, Turner proposed increasing the deposits on aluminum cans and bottles so people would pick up more trash. "Those 1,000 people we let go—it would give them something to do."[48]

Turner brought the following assets to Time Warner collection of companies:

FILM AND TV PRODUCTION

Castle Rock Entertainment

New Line Cinema

Turner Pictures

Hanna-Barbera Cartoons

TV AND CABLE CHANNELS

Cable News Network, CNN International, and Headline News channels

CNN Airport Network

Turner Network Television (TNT)

Turner Classic Movies channel

Cartoon Network

WTBS, an Atlanta station carried on cable nationwide (The Superstation is the most-watched network on cable television, reaching 71 million homes.)[49]

Interests in a regional sports network and a German news network

FILM LIBRARIES

MGM/United Artists films

Older Warner Brothers movies and certain RKO films

TV programs and cartoons

OTHER BUSINESSES

Atlanta Braves baseball team

Atlanta Hawks basketball team (96 percent interest)

Atlanta Thrashers Hockey Team

World Championship Wrestling

CNN Center, and Atlanta office and Omni hotel complex

Home video

Publishing[50]

~

At the start of the merger, there were reports that some Time Warner executives dismissed Turner as an accidental success, attributing his achievements to dumb luck. On the other hand, others welcomed Turner as a shrewd, visionary leader.

A television agent for Creative Artists Agency said of Turner, "In a business that has gotten exceedingly corporate, Ted is one of the few real showmen left. He's very entrepreneurial in a way that harks back to studio moguls of the past."[51]

~

At a New York meeting of television and cable industry leaders shortly after Turner became vice-chairman of Time Warner, Ted responded to the frequently asked question "How can someone who's been his own boss for 35 years go to work for someone else?"

"Well, when I married Jane Fonda, I mean, I was taking on a real risk there, too. 'Cause she's got a lot of ideas, and she doesn't exactly toe the party line, you know."

Turner's voice went up an octave:

"She goes, 'I don't wanna go to that movie,' or 'I

don't wanna go to that restaurant.'" Turner paused. "Yes, dear."

"Well, if I can do that I can probably live with the executives of Time Warner. At least they let me go home at night, and I get a few hours a day when I'm free and I can do whatever I want."[52]

~

Turner oversees the following properties within Time Warner:

HBO

Cinemax

CNN

TNT

TBS Superstation

Cartoon Network

Turner Classic Movies

New Line Cinema and Fine Line

Castle Rock Entertainment

~

In 1996 there was speculation that shareholders might push for Turner to replace Gerry Levin as chairman, if he wanted the job. Major Time Warner shareholders felt it was Levin's fault that the stock had performed badly for four years. Edgar Bronfman Jr., chairman of Seagrams, Gordon Crawford, a media investor at Capital Research and Management, and

Malone of TCI were said to be among the dissident shareholders. TCI and Seagrams each control 9 percent of Time Warner stock.

~

Turner acknowledged problems with a laggard share price but showed no signs of making a move on the chairman's job:

"At Time Warner, we're all pissed off. We're the Rodney Dangerfield of the entertainment world. Godammit, I'm like the guy in Network—*we own it—I'm as mad as hell. We're going to get some respect around here one of these days. I tell [Gerald Levin], we're like Tsar Nicholas and his family, behind the gates of St. Petersburg. And there are the angry shareholders. And all we have is [now deceased Time Warner CEO] Steve Ross's aging security guard to keep 'em out until we get things straightened out. Don't lose your sense of humor, especially when the stock's down."*[53]

~

Turner reassured shareholders:

"We're doing fine. There are always problems when you get married, right? But if you have a good attitude and you want to be married—and we are. . . . When I was chairman of Turner Broadcasting I tried to be the best chairman I could. And now I'm trying to be the best vice-chairman I can. It's a big difference."[54]

THE TURNER STYLE

STUDY THE PAST, LIVE IN THE FUTURE

In the mid-1980s a CNN executive said of Turner, "Ted's mind is always five or ten years down the road. Right now he's probably living in 1995."[1]

~

Asked if he was happier during his campaign to become one of America's top yachtsmen than he was at the moment, Turner explained: "Well, I keep moving. I never seem to have time to stop and to reflect on past accomplishments. I'm looking more into the future—there's a hell of a lot still to be done. I'm not about to rest on my laurels. There's a lot of wrongs that need righting. I won't stop and rest until they have all been righted—which means I probably won't stop and rest."[2]

~

"You don't look back, you gotta look ahead."[3]

~

125

Turner looks to his own future but also the future of society:

> *"My main concern is the future of the planet. I have a recurring dream. The world was kind of like Road Warrior. Everything had broken down. Chaos everywhere. Everyone was starving. People had resorted to cannibalism. I think about this all the time. This is the worst case scenario. But I had refused to be a cannibal. I was going to starve to death."[4]*

$\sim$

> *"A visionary is supposed to have a vision of the future. I think I was right most of the time."[5]*

HIRE WELL, THEN DELEGATE

Ted Turner is able to accomplish so much because he manages as he sees the need: He visits his office only a few days every month but calls his executives frequently, reads documents and memos, marks them with his comments, and returns them daily to the office. One colleague noted, "He has a photographic memory. He can glance at a five-page memo and tell you what he doesn't like about paragraph 20, line 4."[6]

$\sim$

> *"I've always been good at delegating authority. I'm letting more of the decisions be made now because we're in so many more areas."[7]*

Asked if anyone could actually manage a company as large as Time Warner, Turner replied: "There's no way a [Sumner] Redstone or [Rupert] Murdoch or whoever can effectively make decisions by themselves involving companies of this size. Decisions have to be made as close to the action as possible. That's how you get diversity of product."[8]

~

WEALTH

Turner admits that when he saw his name on the Forbes' richest Americans list for the first time in 1982, he looked at his ranking and thought, "Hmm, I can do a little better."[9]

~

In 1966 Turner was worth an estimated $2.2 million. Thirty-one years later, in 1997, he was worth approximately $3.2 billion.[10]

"I'm only 56, Rupert Murdoch [64] and Sumner Redstone [71] are the two guys in this business richer than I am. But if the actuarial tables are right, I'll be the richest guy in the business in another ten years."[11]

~

"I've got more stuff than anybody ever had in the history of the world. I have an Indian headdress, and an African outfit, and this set of glass Tiffany

dice. I've got my copy of the America's Cup up here on the mantel, I've got a poster of the MGM lion on a beach. I'm the proud father of three baby bears. My bear Yogi on my plantation just had cubs. I've got a lot of stuff I didn't have before. I've got a dove nesting right here on the windowsill! I've got more awards than anybody—anybody my age. I've probably got more debt than anyone in the world. That's something, isn't it?"[12]

~

"I didn't really set out to make a lot of money, I really didn't, and that has not been my major motivation. . . . I just wanted to see if these things could be done. I felt that had I been born four or five hundred years ago, I would have wanted to be an explorer, like Columbus or Magellan. In fact, I probably would have preferred to do that . . . but I did get to be a kind of pioneer or explorer in the television business."[13]

~

Do Turner's life goals center around material gains?

"Oh no, not at all, I've realized how unimportant materialism is. That's where this country is going wrong. We've become too materialistic and I think television is mainly responsible. Values and achievements are much more important than possessions."[14]

~

"Being a billionaire or being a millionaire or being broke—and I've been all three at one time or another—it doesn't make that much difference. If you've been bitten by the capitalism bug, or the achievement bug, you want to be the best in whatever you do. And [no matter] how much money you have, you don't really have that much time to enjoy it."[15]

~

"There are different gradations of greed. A certain amount of ambition is good. Particularly as long as you play by the rules. You don't steal from your partners. The easiest way in the world to get a few bucks is to go hold up a 7-Eleven store. But that's not the way to the top. That's the way to jail. You have to play by the rules to get the satisfaction."[16]

~

"A lot of people on this Forbes list of the richest people, it's not that they're necessarily stingy or bad people. It's just that they're so busy making money and thinking about how to get more. Because you can't spend billions of dollars. You can only drive one Rolls-Royce at a time. That's $200,000. I drive a Ford. I deliberately keep my life simple. Why? Because I enjoy that. I never really liked ostentatious wealth."[17]

~

"I can't stand snobbery or phoniness, I mean I just can't stand it. It makes me ill."[18]

∽

"I bet you're all wondering what it feels like to be a billionaire. It's disappointing, really. I remember when it happened to me. I'd been watching the value of my stocks climb, and I realized that when they hit a certain point, I'd become a billionaire. On the day they hit, I was so excited. I wanted to tell someone. But who? I couldn't tell my employees. They'd say, 'Great. Now pay me more money.' I couldn't tell my friends. They weren't nearly as wealthy as I was. So that evening I told my wife [his second wife, Janie] as the kids were running around. She said, 'That's great, but I have to deal with the kids right now.' I've learned since then that great wealth isn't nearly as good as average sex."[19]

∽

On an ABC-TV *Primetime Live* interview with Turner, Sam Donaldson suggested that making money is just a way of keeping score. Turner replied: "And not a very good one. I think it would be tragic to just be remembered for making a lot of money. But basically, having a huge amount of wealth, I like to liken it to eating popcorn. It fills you up, but it's not as satisfying. If you have a strong philanthropic component in your life, I mean, you never see someone who— who lives a life of service committing suicide. The people who commit suicide are ones that are basically selfish."[20]

~

Teddy Turner, Turner's son, described trying to buy gifts for his parents' birthdays: "They're very, very hard to buy for. It's not about the money, it's about the thought. And the uniqueness. And he's very practical."[21]

~

Once he became truly wealthy, Turner knew what he wanted to do next:

"I consider myself the luckiest man in the world. I've achieved everything I've set out to achieve. . . . I'm going to dedicate the rest of my life to doing what I can for the rest of the world. You know, one area where we've really failed in American society is that we've conned everybody into thinking that if you're rich, you're going to be happy."[22]

POWER

"I'd feel powerful if my kids got straight A's and my wife never got mad at me and I never got a case of diarrhea. As it is, power is a bunch of hooey."[23]

~

When Ted Turner launched CNN in Europe, there was considerable opposition to the expansion from members of the European Community. Among other names, Turner was called an imperialist and an ugly American. The name-calling seemed overblown to Turner:

"I don't want to upset the apple cart or make any-body mad. I just want to be a banana, one of the bunch."[24]

～

". . . I'm nice to the average guy. I understand him. The average guy has to be nice or he'll get shit on. Only the rich can afford to be shits."[25]

～

Yet Turner does have power, and power has its per-quisites. As chief of CNN, when Turner calls to set up a meeting, world leaders answer.

After a 1986 trip to Cuba to visit President Fidel Castro, Turner showed his photo album to a reporter:

"Here's the great Commie dictator we're so worried about—having a hot toddy! Ha! And look, here's the great Commie dictator in his bare feet!"[26]

～

"Here's us hunting. Twenty-two attempts on [Castro's] life by the CIA and I'm sitting next to him with a loaded rifle? . . . I could have shot him in the back!"[27]

～

Turner called Fidel Castro his "First Commie buddy":

"Communism is fine with me. It's part of the fabric of life on this planet. The United States is only 5 percent of the world's population. I'm in global politics already."[28]

~

"I'm the only man on the planet ever to fly on Cuba's Air Force One *with their president and on America's* Air Force One *with our president."[29]*

~

In December 1997 Ted Turner, along with Jane Fonda, met with Fidel Castro again as part of the couple's visit to CNN's bureau in Havana. The Atlanta-based news network was the first U.S. news organization to open a Havana bureau after relations between the United States and Cuba began to thaw somewhat following the end of the Cold War.[30]

~

During his sailing days, Turner rubbed Docksiders with distinguished company. Prince Harold of Norway and his father King Olav, King Juan Carlos of Spain, and King Constantine of Greece were among the crowned heads of Europe who enjoyed sailing with a man they considered the quintessential American.[31]

After a victory banquet in Stockholm, Turner rose to say a few words:

"Well, there are sure a lot of kings in this room. But where I come from, every man is a king."[32]

FAME

After winning the America's Cup, Turner noted:

"Fame is like love. You can never have too much of it."[33]

~

Gary Jobson said that during the 1977 America's Cup challenge, Turner became obsessed with the publicity he was receiving. This made life difficult for Jobson, who was Turner's number-two man aboard the *Courageous*: "One of the tough things was that Ted never listened if I felt the need to talk about myself for a minute. He only listened when I talked about him. It got pretty far out. One Sunday in July, we stopped at three newsstands on the way to the boat to find *Time* and *Newsweek*. He read about himself in *Newsweek*, then asked me to read the coverage in *Time* to him. We were ten minutes late getting to the dock. He would have a fit if the morning papers didn't arrive at the house on time."[34]

~

Just before he made a $1 billion donation to the United Nations, Turner received the ultimate validation of his fame. Sculptors from Madame Tussaud's Wax Museum in London took his measurements for an effigy.[35]

~

Fame may not have bothered Turner at first, but like most celebrities, as his fame grows, his privacy diminishes. More and more in recent years he has withdrawn to remote mountain ranches where he can live, work, fly fish, and horseback ride away from crowds. When Ted and Jane Fonda bought their huge ranch in the Patagonia region of Argentina, Turner told a local newspaper that he bought the vast natural reserve to have a place where they could go to rest in privacy and safety.[36]

THE DEMON
WITHIN

FEELING A LITTLE WACKO

Ted Turner was once asked if he goes out of his way to be outrageous:

> *"Hell, no. There's a fine line between being colorful and being an asshole, and I hope I'm still just colorful. Do you think I'm wacko? I'm feeling a bit weird right now."*[1]

~

Some of Turner's behavioral extremes could stem from his enormous physical and mental energy:

> *"The worst sin, the ultimate sin for me, in anything, is to be bored."*[2]

~

In 1985 Turner sought the help of a therapist who prescribed the mood-regulating drug lithium. As usual, Turner made no secret of the fact that he was taking a medication.

J. J. Ebaugh, the woman for whom he left his second wife, Janie, described the change lithium made in Ted Turner's moods. "Before, it was pretty scary to be around the guy sometimes because you never knew what in the world was going to happen next," said Ebaugh. "If he was about to fly off the handle, you just never knew. That's why the whole world was on pins and needles around him. But with lithium he became very even tempered. Ted's just one of those miracle cases. I mean, lithium is great stuff, but in Ted's particular case, lithium is a miracle."[3]

~

Sam Donaldson, in a 1997 *ABC-TV Primetime Live* interview, asked Turner if he had been treated for bouts of depression.

Turner: "No, that's incorrect."

Donaldson: "You haven't?"

Turner: "I've had ups and downs. But—but I do not—I don't suffer from depression. I'm not on any medication."

Donaldson: "You took lithium until the mid-'80s."

Turner: "Well, I was misdiagnosed by—I was misdiagnosed. I took it for a couple of years, and I didn't notice any difference. And when I—when I was diagnosed by the head of the psychiatric department at Emory [University] as part of a normal checkup, he said I shouldn't be—there was nothing wrong with me and I should stop taking it. And I did, and I haven't noticed any difference since then. And that was over a year ago."

Donaldson then asked if Turner had wild mood swings.

Turner: "I have moderate mood swings. I have normal mood swings."

Donaldson: "I read the story you've walked through the CNN offices, yelling, jumping on desks. I have a certain sympathy for this."

Turner: "I've never once jumped on a desk in my life."[4]

NOTE: Turner may have a valid point. There are many documented accounts of Turner's high moods, yet except for an episode when he suffered from chronic fatigue syndrome, there are few accounts of prolonged down moods.[5]

MIXED MORALITY

Considering that he sometimes uses raw language and behaves outrageously himself, it surprises some people that Turner objects to depictions of crude or violent behavior on the public airwaves.

While Ted sermonized against the corrupting effects of movies like *Taxi Driver*, he readily admitted that he liked pictures of nude women and even made some pornographic movies of his own, in which he starred.[6]

The movie *Crash*, produced by the Canadian David Cronenberg, which depicted people being sexually aroused by car wrecks, won a special jury prize at the 1996 Cannes Film Festival for its "audacity and daring and originality." When Turner objected to showing *Crash* on TNT because he found its theme offensive, he was accused of being heavy-handed.

"[Turner] did what amounts to behind-the-scenes censorship of my movie," said a livid Cronenberg, "which I resent, to say the least."[7]

"It's very reminiscent of Jesse Helms," said the film's star, Helen Hunt. "Ted Turner's moral fascism has no place in the entertainment industry."[8]

Turner however, remained steadfast in his views:

"The test of a program in my mind is, is this a program that you would be proud and happy to have your children sit and watch, and is it a program that if your mother and father saw it and knew that you were responsible for putting it on the air, would they be proud of you?"[9]

"I yanked it [Crash] off the schedule, it bothered me. . . . The people with warped minds are gonna like it, though. I mean, it's really weird. . . . Imagine the first teenager who decides to have sex while driving a hundred miles an hour, and probably the movie will get 'em to do that."[10]

According to some reports, Turner also was repulsed by child molestation and abuse scenes in the movie *Bastard Out of Carolina* and discouraged New Line and Fine Line from buying the film and releasing it. Executives at TNT deny that Turner intervened in their decision regarding the movie.

Turner appears to be concerned more with the standard cable TV fare that comes straight into homes as part of the basic cable package. He objects to children having easy access to depictions of child abuse, rape, and other forms of violence and brutality. He seems to have greater tolerance for the movies shown by HBO, Cinemax, and channels that people select and pay an extra fee to view.

> *"I'm not for any form of news censorship, but I don't think movies are news."[11]*

Turner always has objected to gratuitous violence on television but says in recent years he doesn't monitor the content of his networks as much as he once did:

> *"The bigger I've gotten and the more successful . . . the more that my standards have been compromised for the sake of the almighty dollar. . . . My networks run a lot of programming that I'm not happy about and it bothers me. But does it bother me enough to do anything about it? No, it doesn't."[12]*

Turner still maintains that other networks depict more violence than his channels do:

> *"They'll do anything to be tops in the ratings race. One of them said to me, 'Ted, you are forever criticizing network people for not having any principles about what we put on the air. But I want you to know that a lot of us are very moral people in our private lives.' 'Whoopee,' I said 'that's what the Nazis claimed when they went home at night from their work in the gas chambers.'"[13]*

~

Turner has known Moral Majority leader Jerry Falwell for a long time. Falwell once said of Turner, "He has the greatest potential for good of any man I ever met."[14]

~

> *"I abhor violence when it's taking another person's life, but a little violence in the rink or on the football field is OK. The worst they do is knock each other down. That's what men really enjoy, anyway: getting together and beating the shit out of each other."[15]*

~

As much as he dislikes war, Turner has supported and even played a role in Civil War documentaries such as *Gettysburg.*

John Frankenheimer, director of TNT's graphic Civil War movie *Andersonville* says, "My experience with Ted was extremely supportive. No interference whatsoever. He's a very filmmaker-friendly guy. If you guys make him come off as some kind of ogre, I think that's all wrong."[16]

～

If Turner's moral rules puzzle some people, so does his budget-consciousness. Despite the large sums he's paid for sailing campaigns and the prices he's been willing to pay to acquire companies or real estate, he can be cheap. Turner, apparently, is obsessively frugal; he used to cut his own hair, shine his own shoes, and flew tourist class, even when his ballplayers were traveling first class. Unlike other skippers, he did not pay any of his yacht crews' expenses during the America's Cup.[17]

On the other hand, in the mid-1970s Turner was spending about $100,000 a year buying or refitting boats and transporting himself, his crews, and boats to various places on the international racing circuit.[18]

～

Turner admits to some inconsistency and some faults but says at least he strives to be honest:

"In the world of the blind, the one-eyed man is king."[19]

～

Whatever his moral and ethical positions, Turner apparently follows the biblical admonition to treat his body as a temple:

"I take vitamins. I try not to eat starches, don't eat desserts, try to stay away from sweets and between-

meal snacks, and I brush with Crest twice a day, for God's sake."[20]

SORRY, SORRY, SORRY

During his lifetime Ted Turner has made many public apologies:

> *"I get in a lot of trouble when there's press around. Mostly at cocktail parties is when I get in trouble. If you had as much to say as I do, you'd get in trouble too."*[21]

~

Turner has apologized for saying that Christianity is for losers, for comparing Australian media mogul Rupert Murdoch to Adolf Hitler, and for suggesting that unemployed Blacks be used to haul mobile missiles, "like Egyptians building the pyramids." He also has offended many people by insisting that the Ten Commandments are badly out of date and that the "Star-Spangled Banner" is too warlike and difficult to sing and should be dumped as the U.S. national anthem.[22]

~

Turner and media mogul Rupert Murdoch compete in several television markets, and the clash between the two men was emotional, to say the least:

> *"[Murdoch] is the only guy who gets my dander up. ... I like everybody else now that Hitler's dead."*[23]

Perhaps it was accumulated stress, perhaps it was a phase of his life, but during the 1977 America's Cup races, Turner made an unusually large number of apologies.

When they worked on the dock or walked through town, Turner and his crew routinely greeted attractive women by throwing up their own shirts and demanding "Show me your tits."[24]

During the competition, some people in Newport wore lapel pins saying "Beat the Mouth." Turner spotted a man wearing such a button at the Castle Hill restaurant and challenged the fellow to go outside and beat him right then and there. Later Turner apologized to the restaurant manager for making a fuss but insisted the button was unfair.

According to another story, Turner got drunk, made a pass at a younger woman in his wife's presence, and then slipped out of the party early, leaving Janie Turner to find her own way home. Turner said that he'd been invited out for the evening by social climbers that he barely knew and that dinner was delayed as the hosts squired him around introducing him to their friends as if he were an old friend. Turner admitted getting annoyed and having a conversation with a younger woman but says anyone would have been ill-tempered in the situation. As he explained the matter, Turner dug a deeper hole:

"One of the most popular stories that came out was that I had said something about being willing to fix up some old broads who needed to get drilled. Now does that sound like me? I don't like drilling old broads."[25]

~

The head of Turner's America's Cup syndicate insisted that Ted write a letter of apology to the private club where the incident occurred.

His apology began:

"It has come to my attention that conduct at the party July 2nd at the Sprouting Rock Beach Association may have been bothersome to some of your fine members. If this is the case, I wish to apologize profusely because I certainly did have a couple of drinks too many that Saturday night."[26]

John Winslow, the club president, replied to Turner's note, saying that no complaint had been filed against Turner, so the club would take no action: Winslow then added:

Your letter reminds me of the story of President Lincoln and his cabinet. Several cabinet members complained that General Grant drank too much. After thinking a few minutes President Lincoln replied, "Find out the brand of whiskey he drinks and give it to the other generals."

We do hope that you realize that you and your lovely wife and children are always welcome at the Beach.[27]

145

Even so, Turner curtailed his social life for the remainder of the race. When the race was over and Turner had won, he celebrated wildly, drinking so much that during the victory ceremony, he is said to have slipped under the table drunk. Turner denies that he passed out. He says he merely reached under the table to pick up something he'd dropped.

～

During one America's Cup competition Turner declared: "If being against stuffiness and pompousness and bigotry is bad behavior, then I plead guilty."[28]

～

After winning the America's Cup, Turner was invited to be a guest on the *Dick Cavett Show*. Turner was exhausted from the victory celebration and from dealing with business issues that had piled up during the racing season. He arrived at the studio only to be kept waiting while Cavett finished up an earlier taping.

Cavett asked Turner several questions related to his image as "Mouth of the South," then got right to the point.

"Let's not leave viewers with a false impression," said Cavett. "You are a colorful, boisterous, sometimes inebriated playboy type. Maybe it's an act or it's created by the press, but that is your image. You wouldn't deny that, would you?"

"I have heard that you are a little twinkle-toed TV announcer," Turner shot back. "Would you deny that?"

Cavett then went on to ask about the time Turner fired a Braves' traveling secretary over excessive expense accounts.

"Wasn't he a midget?" asked Cavett.

"Yes. He's the only midget I've fired in my twenty years in business."

"Didn't you have a good line about that?"

"I said, 'Put him up on a desk so I can look him in the eye and fire him.' But it wasn't my line. If so, I'd have your job and you'd have mine."[29]

The interview ended and the show never aired.

$\sim$

Probably the best that can be said for Turner's runaway mouth is that he is an equal opportunity offender. When a coalition of black citizens in Charlotte, South Carolina, contested the broadcast license of WRET TV because the station didn't hire enough minorities, Turner met with the group and won then over with a simple observation:

"You know, I don't blame you guys for being mad at me. I'd be mad at me too. But it looks like you got the same problem I've got in my company. You don't have any blacks in high places either. You got three guys [attorneys] here who are doin' all the talking— and they're all white."[30]

$\sim$

What would Ted Turner say if he ever met the Pope? Turner answered that question with a question. "Ever seen a Polish mine detector?" and then raised his foot. He continued to say that Pope John Paul II should "get with it—welcome to the 20th century," and among other things abolish the biblical commandment against adultery.

After that comment, a spokesman said that Turner "regrets any offense his comments may have caused . . . and extends his heartfelt apologies."[31]

~

During a speech at the awards banquet for the National Sportswriters and Sportscasters Association, Turner tried to explain why he didn't like baseball agent Jerry Kapstein:

"After all, you should have some reason to dislike a guy besides the fact he wears a full-length fur coat and is a Jew."[32]

~

When Turner found himself unable to purchase a broadcast network, he compared himself to a victim of the Holocaust:

"I feel like the Jewish people in Germany in 1942. I know exactly what it is to be rounded up and sent to the East somewhere. Resettled."

The Anti-Defamation League pointed out to Turner that he was making light of the suffering of millions of people. Ted apologized, saying "I respect the heritage of all people. I now realize that my remarks regarding the Holocaust trivialized the tragedy perpetrated on the Jewish people."[33]

～

After Turner's TBS Superstation aired the pro-choice documentary *Abortion: For Survival*, the program was denounced by anti-abortion groups. In an outburst at a press conference, Turner called the anti-abortionists "bozos." Later he said: "I was answering a question as Citizen Turner, I was not answering it as Ted Turner, president of Turner Broadcasting. I was really sorry that I used that term. These people [anti-abortionists] talk about adoption as an alternative. That is a bunch of bull. The biggest problem we have in the world is the population explosion. There are 100 million kids in the world that are up for adoption right now. Adopt them."[34]

～

Turner apologized to Chinese student leader Shen Tong for defending the Beijing government's violent repression of demonstrators in Tiananmen Square. During an appearance in Beijing, he had said, in part: "Certainly we all know that weeks went by and repeated warnings were given to the students to go home. They were breaking the law."[35]

Turner added that the Chinese government deserved as much sympathy as the students. "We would accomplish more by saying that a tragedy has occurred in the world and we bleed in our hearts for the students and others who were killed and hurt, but we also bleed for those in government and those soldiers who felt they were forced to take that action."[36]

Critics suggested that by going easy on the Chinese government, Turner may have been protecting his business interests. Turner's TNT & Cartoon Network launched a 24-hour cartoon and film channel in China in 1994.[37]

∼

Turner has made other comments for which he did not apologize, but some people believe he should have. In a 1996 speech to a forum of international journalists hosted by CNN, Turner said: "The United States has got some of the dumbest people in the world. I want you to know that. We know that. It's a disgrace. I mean there are times when I have been so discouraged about my own country."[38]

∼

Despite some appalling statements, associates say Turner's utterances, even when hurtful, flow from his mouth without malice. He treats people fairly and without prejudice. And despite his gaffes, Turner plows right ahead with his life:

"I don't spend a whole lot of time reviewing myself at all. I'm too busy moving to be viewing."[39]

SO MANY GAFFES, SO FEW ENEMIES

How can Turner go through life doing and saying such outrageous things yet find people who are willing to work with him and share their lives with him?

"What business guys like about Turner is that he's been there, done it all, and doesn't give a damn what people think," noted an IBM executive.[40]

~

University president Vartan Gregorian said of Turner, "Chutzpah he has plenty, but hubris he has not."[41]

~

"Ted likes to make his points with overstatement," observed a Turner insider, "but if you look real close, there's always a grain of truth there."[42]

~

Dee Woods, Turner's longtime secretary, has been one of his biggest fans. "I'm crazy about him," Woods said. "People only see one side of him, but he's multi-faceted and I probably see more of the facets than most people. He's an environmentalist. He is starting a campaign against nuclear war. He wants to start a foundation to work for a better society. He is more intelligent than most people imagine. By some people's standards he may be a good ol' boy, but I'll tell you one thing, he is an incredibly smart good ol' boy."[43]

~

Jane Fonda, Turner's third wife, observed: "I've never met anybody who can so quickly recognize a truth and internalize it. When he feels something is right, he just does it. Without a backward look."[44]

~

George Babick, head of CNN's New York sales office in 1980, gave some advice about his boss Turner: "If Ted predicted the sun will come up in the west tomorrow morning, you'd laugh and say he's full of it. But you'd still set the alarm. You wouldn't want to miss the miracle."[45]

~

Quite simply, noted J. J. Ebaugh, one of Turner's former girlfriends: "Ted's the most interesting guy in the world."[46]

A HIGH-MAINTENANCE GUY

"When I was 17 I had written a suicide note, and I was standing on the fifth-floor ledge at Read House in Chattanooga, ready to jump. It was over a girl. Then I thought, if I jump now, it's all over. Maybe I should jump tomorrow. After that I decided women are like streetcars. If you miss one, another one comes along."[47]

~

Turner once claimed that men are natural polyga-mists, and he didn't restrain himself:

"I didn't like being alone when I was on the road."[48]

◠

"I don't like sleeping alone. I like the patter of little bare feet in the morning. I like people too much."[49]

◠

Turner had numerous girlfriends at CNN. A former executive remembers walking down the hall and seeing Turner's ex-wife Jane, Barbara Pyle (a photog-rapher who also produced CNN documentaries), Liz Wickersham (*Playboy* cover girl and an on-air announcer at CNN), and J. J. Ebaugh (who served as Turner's pilot and advisor on environmental issues) all talking together and realized that "they had all slept with Ted. I couldn't help wondering if they were comparing notes."[50]

◠

Turner was upset with a *Playboy* writer who reported that Turner had taken pornographic photographs of himself and his sex partners:

Turner: "You know I was really pissed off about my first *Playboy Interview* when it came out. You lied to me; you said you were not going to run anything like that."
Reporter: "Like what?"

Turner: "We were going to leave women out of
it. You know, I bared my soul. I gave you
everything I had and only asked that you
didn't take any cheap shots."[51]

~

Jane Fonda apparently had heard the stories about
Ted Turner before they married:

"I have to give Jane credit," said a Turner executive who knows the couple well. "She's figured Ted
out pretty well. He never could be alone, he couldn't
stand it. So he never was. Even when he was married,
he always had a girl with him. Jane never leaves him
alone. They're always together. It's probably the only
time in his life he's been with only one woman."[52]

FAMILY VALUES

SHE AIN'T MUCH, BUT SHE'S ALL I GOT

During his sailing years Ted Turner said, "My priorities are in order. I've never had any problem with priorities. Mine are sailing, business, and family, in that order. Don't you imagine a lot of guys who wouldn't admit it feel that way? Sailing, business, and family. That's why I succeed so well at stuff other people don't give a shit about."[1]

~

Years later, at his youngest daughter's college graduation ceremony, Turner had updated his point of view:

"Something I've learned—I'm sharing my deepest experiences with you—is when you get married, really get books or get some counseling, because schools don't teach you about marriage. At least, my experience was I didn't get enough teaching. I had two failed marriages and it caused a lot of trouble for my children and everything else. Here I am at fifty, I'm now going and getting counseling and try-

ing to learn. If I had done it earlier, I'm sure I would have had a lot happier life, and the women I lived with would have been a lot happier too.[2]

~

After he was expelled from college and just before he went to work for his father's business in Macon, Georgia, Turner and Judy Nye were married. She was a champion sailor whom Ted met at a boating competition. Commodore of the Northwestern University sailing team, Judy is the daughter of Harry Nye, one of the founders of Murphy & Nye Sailmakers.

~

Ted and Judy's marriage was turbulent from the start, but they often sailed together. On one occasion the couple competed separately in the same Y-Flyer race, and Judy was in the lead. Ted came from behind and rammed her boat in order to knock her out of the event and win the race himself.

The Turners already had one daughter when they separated and divorced, but they made a second try and were living together as common-law husband and wife at the time their second child, Teddy, was born. After the sailing incident, Turner's first wife left him for good.

Even the separation was turbulent. Turner took custody of the children, refusing to allow their mother to visit even after a court-ordered visitation. Judy didn't see the children again for 12 years.[3]

~

By then Turner had moved to Atlanta to run his business. It was there that he met Jane Shirley Smith, a Delta Airlines flight attendant. They were married June 2, 1964, but that marriage did not have an auspicious beginning:

At the wedding reception Turner told some friends: "I didn't really want to get married. I didn't want to marry Janie. I said I'd marry her because she was pregnant—but don't expect me to be a good husband."[4]

~

Ted and the first Jane had three children, two sons and a daughter:

"Ted named them. Yes, Rhett is named for Rhett Butler, Beauregard, or Beau, as we call him, is named for General Beauregard. He wanted to name Jennie Scarlett, after Scarlett O'Hara. But I wouldn't let him—I thought that would be a little too much for her to live up to. Then he decided to name her Jeanie, after Stephen Foster's song 'Jeanie with the Light Brown Hair.' But I changed it to 'Jennie.'"[5]

~

At a press conference during the 1977 America's Cup, there was speculation as to how Turner and the skipper of the *Australia* would have fared if they had switched boats:

"We're used to our boat, our sails, our rig. Noel is used to his. It's like asking Noel Robins or me what

would happen if we switched wives. Noel is used to his wife and he likes her better than mine. And I like mine better than his." Turner paused, then added, "*She ain't much, but she's all I got.*"[6]

～

Turner introduced his wife Janie to some acquaintances, when someone said, "You sure have a beautiful woman there." Turner responded: "Yup, and if she doesn't stay beautiful, the next one will be even better."[7]

～

Despite many problems, including Turner's long absences from home to participate in sailing events, Ted and Janie Turner remained married for 24 years.

A neighbor and family friend said that Janie Turner preferred a private life, centered around her children, church, and friends, and after a while she and Ted simply went their separate ways: "He's not really a nice person, the way he played around on his wife. He was very raw, very crude about it, but I don't think Janie put up with it for the money or the easy life. I really don't think she ever cared about the money. I think she really loved him. Or thought she did."[8]

～

Turner had extramarital affairs, but none seemed to threaten his marriage until he met J. J. Ebaugh in Newport Rhode Island in 1980 during his third participation in the America's Cup yacht race. Their relationship lasted until 1986.

~

After his first wife left him, Turner pursued her diligently and won her back, but then returned to his old, unfaithful ways. Later, when Ebaugh broke off their relationship, he abruptly left a safari vacation with his sons to persuade her to come back to him.

Ebaugh, who bears a striking resemblance to Jane Fonda, was finally persuaded. Turner left Janie and set up housekeeping with J. J. in Roswell, a trendy community on the rural fringes of Atlanta, and at a cliffside home in Big Sur, California.[9]

> *"It's changed a lot in the last year. I mean, when you leave your wife of 23 years and run off with a 30-year-old woman, that changes things. I've been hopping a little more."*[10]

~

When Turner was asked if his impending divorce would have an effect on his business decisions, he replied:

> *"Well, I haven't been divorced in a long time, but I was separated from my wife for a year, and we are discussing a divorce. It's a major consideration. Divorces are not cheap. It was something that needed to be taken into consideration. That was one of the reasons for the stock split."*[11]

~

After Turner's divorce from Janie, he spent more time away from the office and on his ranches. He also began seeing a counselor. An associate said, "He's much mellower now, he doesn't yell at people."

Turner put it this way: "I am maturing. That's better than aging. You enjoy different things."[12]

In time, however, the relationship with Ebaugh also ended.[13]

SPEAK UP, KIDS, MAKE YOURSELF HEARD

Janie Turner has said that when Ted was home, the family went to bed at 9 P.M. if he said so, and each morning he expected to have the children seated at the breakfast table by 8 A.M.[14]

Turner's son Teddy once recalled: "Dad was often away in those days [when he was creating CNN]. When he was home, there was a lot of yelling and tension and getting smacked around. I never could decide which was worse—having him away a lot or having him home."[15]

∼

Turner followed his father's philosophy:

"I wanted it to be harder for my sons than other kids."[16]

∼

Teddy recalls a canoe trip he took with his young stepbrothers and his father. His dad, he said, "yelled and screamed the whole time. It was a nightmare. So when we had finished and we were just going down the Chattahoochee River and Dad said, 'Well, did everybody have a great time?' I said no. And, boy he smacked me hard."[17]

~

"If he caught you crying," Teddy Turner said, "that was the worst thing you could do. You never expressed your feelings at our house. I was a fairly disturbed child. Dad didn't have time for me. It's only in the last two years we've started to have a real relationship."[18]

~

When the children were small, the Turner family attended an Atlanta Braves' game together. Since they didn't see him much, the youngsters were vying for the attention of their father. One of the younger boys burst into tears, and Janie Turner moved him down to sit next to Ted. Apparently the child was crying because he felt he'd finished last in the competition for attention. Turner tried to console the boy:

"Well, son, I've only been paying attention to those who talked the loudest, and I guess I didn't hear you. You've got to speak up, son. Make yourself heard. I'm sorry, son. It's been a rough summer for me. You know how it is when you're playing ball, huh?"[19]

~

When Ted's father had challenged him not to take a drink until he finished college, Ted lost the challenge. However, Turner promised his own son Teddy that if he would stay sober until after finishing college, he would give him $15,000. "It's the only thing I ever beat my father at," Teddy said.[20]

~

Teddy Turner became a television cameraman, working for CNN in the Moscow bureau. Returning from a bar late one night, the vehicle in which Turner was riding spun out on the ice and hit a pole. Young Ted was seriously injured and was transported home from Russia by air ambulance. He later said it was the turning point, when he and his father began to get closer.[21]

JANE FONDA'S HUSBAND

Turner's life again changed dramatically when he married for the third time:

> *"I'm the luckiest man alive! I can't believe I'm married to Jane Fonda!"*[22]

~

Turner and Academy Award–winning actress Jane Fonda were wed in December 1991, at Avalon, Turner's 8,100-acre plantation near Tallahassee, Florida. Jimmy Brown was best man and Troy Hayden, 18, gave his mother away. Between them Ted and Jane had accumulated four previous marriages and seven children.

Fonda has a daughter, Vanessa Vadim, whose father is the movie director Roger Vadim. Her son, Troy, is a child from her marriage to California political activist and politician Tom Hayden.

~

When Turner married Jane Fonda, he proclaimed: "I am happy I have finally met a woman who is my equal."[23]

~

At a belated wedding reception for Ted and Jane in Los Angeles at L'Orangerie restaurant, Dolly Parton toasted them as ". . . the Man of the Year. The Woman of the Hour. The Couple of the Century."[24]

~

Biographer Porter Bibb said of Turner and Fonda: "They have an incredible union of two radical overachievers."[25]

~

Not everyone thought of the Turner/Fonda marriage as made in heaven: One of Jane Fonda's close friends complained, "In marrying Turner, she made a pact with the Devil. She sold out."[26]

~

Some of Turner's Southern buddies were appalled when he courted Fonda. "They were pretty shocked when he married 'Hanoi Jane.'" A friend of Ted's explained, "There was a real undercurrent of betrayal. How could he do this? Ted, the great embodiment of the American capitalist system, how could he marry her?"[27]

～

Turner asked his friends to give Fonda a chance. She is:

"The right woman at last. Jane Fonda was right about Vietnam, I was wrong."[28]

～

In some ways, Turner and Fonda have parallel histories, including strong-willed fathers and a parent who committed suicide. Jane's mother slit her own throat with a razor blade after Henry Fonda left her for another woman. Henry Fonda told his children that their mother had died of a heart attack. Jane learned the truth from Brooke Hayward, a childhood friend whose mother, the actress Margaret Sullivan, had been Henry Fonda's first wife:

"I'm sure those of us who've had powerful parental figures looming over our lives, whether famous or not, have had to find our way to a clearing of sorts" said Jane Fonda, "where we're not crowded by their shadow, and to work it through, to make our peace, and to see them laughing in our dreams."[29]

～

Fonda noted of Turner: "Oh, he's very much like my father, with none of the bad parts . . . one big difference, Ted is well within his skin. Ted is not afraid of expressing need, and he loves women, and he is not threatened by them."[30]

~

"Ted has huge arms that he opens up to lots of people that he doesn't necessarily agree with, and I watch them change as a result of it," said Jane. "He's got an expression, 'You can catch more bees with honey,' or whatever that expression is. I feel like this is what I've been preparing for my whole life."[31]

~

Said Turner, of his relationship with Fonda: "We have a community of interests. She's certainly been working on these issues longer than I have, but I've been working on them very hard in the past decade."[32]

~

Even so, Turner and Fonda have had their differences, especially on the subject of gender roles:

"When we were first going out, we had these discussions about women being equal. I told her I didn't think they were equal, I thought they were different. Finally we settled on their being 'roughly equivalent.'"[33]

~

The couple caused quite a stir when they were heard loudly arguing in the ballroom of the Waldorf-Astoria

Hotel in New York—loud enough that the crowd in the room fell silent. Turner went to the podium and apologized: "As you can see, my wife and I are having a discussion, and I want to finish it."

The couple hastily made for the exit.[34]

～

Although he claims to have matured in recent years, Turner still has trouble keeping his mouth shut. After a corporate board meeting at Turner's Flying D ranch, Turner showed the board members around his ranch, pointing out places where he and Jane had been intimate.

"We did it on this rock here, and under that tree, and over there. . . ."[35]

～

Fonda has given up making movies for now, to spend more time with Turner. She says it is entirely possible for a woman to remain strong and a feminist and to devote time to husband and family. "Ted and I met late in our life. We don't have a whole lot of time to savor our happiness, and the idea of taking time away from that to make a movie really doesn't appeal to me that much right now, at least for the moment."[36]

～

The tabloid newspapers have printed reports of a split between Ted and Jane, although the stories have not been confirmed. A source in Atlanta said the couple still seem "to be a unit." Turner once described himself as:

"Jane Fonda's last husband."[37]

DOING THE RIGHT THING

As trustees of the Turner Foundation, the Turner children met, along with Jane Fonda, to vote on a number of environmental grant proposals. Teddy recalls, "We figured it was all set up and he would be 'Dad' like dads do. I can remember the first vote we outvoted Dad on, we thought it was the end of the world. But he thought it was the greatest thing. I think it was part of the transition he wanted—'Think on your own; do the right thing. Because I'm not always going to be here to tell you what to do.'"[38]

~

All the Turner children are now grown.

Laura Lee, his oldest daughter, was married several years ago in one of Atlanta's most publicized weddings. Jennie Turner Garlington, Turner's youngest daughter, is an associate producer of documentaries in CNN's environmental unit.

In 1997 Turner's son Rhett was studying photography at the Rhode Island School of Design.

Turner's son Beau oversees wildlife management on all the Turner properties. That project and his position on the Turner Trust have been important to him: "It's allowed me to do some great things. I think Dad thought it was very, very important to start giving money away while he was still around, so he could see what our interest was in all this. And so he could see his children enjoying the giving."[39]

~

Beau says, "It's amazing when you think about it. My family's one big circus, but we all find a way to get along."

THE RETURN TO IDEALISM

I LOVE EVERYTHING

"I love life, I love the planet, I love my wife, my kids. Animals. I love albatrosses, eagles—chipmunks! I love trees. The redwoods in California!"[1]

Ted Turner grew up hunting and fishing with his father and with Jimmy Brown, and although he relished life out of doors, the condition of the planet was not on his mind until later.

"When he was younger, he wasn't as concerned about the environment," explained Teddy Turner of his father. "It's not like 'Oh, no, that power plant is going to destroy fisheries.' But more than that when we went duck hunting each year, the number of ducks was down. There was no habitat left."[2]

Turner began joining organizations such as Ducks Unlimited, and gradually his awareness and involvement grew. He expressed the problem in terms anyone could understand:

"You can't pave the whole world over with asphalt and still live on it."[3]

〜

"We get more information every day that toxin poisons are a greater threat to us than anyone ever thought. Intelligent people now know that we are really in trouble."[4]

〜

Turner was especially distraught by the dire picture painted in *The Global 2000 Report to the President*, prepared at the request of President Jimmy Carter and published in 1980.[5]

In his concern for the environment, Turner gave up smoking. He banned Styrofoam products from the CNN Center. He hired photographer Barbara Pyle to work on environmental documentaries for television. He refused to use air conditioning, even in the stifling Southern summers.

Sam Donaldson, on a 1997 *Primetime Live* show, asked Turner how he got along without air conditioning:

Turner: "I don't and haven't used it since 1974. I turned the air conditioning off in my home. I figured whether you're wealthy or not, if you're going to be in favor of energy efficiency you have to practice it yourself."

Donaldson: "Well, what do you do in Atlanta, Georgia?"

Turner: "Sweat."[6]

~

Turner is particularly concerned about global warming, as he explained to Larry King of the *Larry King Live* CNN television show.

"Haven't you been outside lately? It's hotter than hell out there! The polar ice caps are melting. I got an island and I know that the ocean is rising, because I watched my beach get washed away."[7]

~

Turner proclaimed that newspapers are doomed, because they take too much energy and natural resources to produce:

"Newspapers are on their way out unless somebody figures out a way to recycle them. They burn so much gasoline delivering the papers in the morning and then the same amount in the afternoon to collect them after they've been read. We just don't have that kind of fuel."[8]

~

Turner says that overpopulation is at the root of many of the environmental problems that are destroying the planet:

"We may be human beings. We may be very smart, but we still have animalistic urges. The goal is to

have as much sex as possible—to have as many children as possible to ensure continuation of your progeny. It's survival of the fittest."[9]

~

"We're giving ourselves cancer from all of the pollution and chemicals we're pumping into our environment and our foods. There's going to be a world food crisis real soon anyway. I mean, if the population keeps exploding. We've got to get a grip on population control before it's too late."[10]

~

"I hate to be a prophet of doom. There's no reason to be hopeless. We can turn this thing around but we have to start now. This is the generation that has to do it. I can help you as much as I can, but I'm getting old."[11]

~

In 1984 Turner led a group of environmentalists in forming the Better World Society. The group's credo was "Harnessing the power of television to make a better world."[12] The organization folded in 1991, but during the six years it existed, it raised almost $12 million and produced approximately 48 documentaries.

"I just care. I'm deeply concerned, we're destroying the planet, that's all. We can save it. We just have to be the best that we can be, rather than the worst."[13]

~

Turner now conducts his environmental activism through the Turner Foundation, where his family serves as directors.

"What's so wonderful," said Turner's daughter Jennie Garlington, "he is our mentor on this whole thing. He will have give us 30 to 40 years of him being a mentor. This is his way of sort of letting us make our mark on the environment, too. It's probably one of the greatest opportunities that any son or daughter can ever hope to have."[14]

~

"In business, he's always been able to see the whole big picture," said Teddy Turner. "What he saw in environmentalism is that the big picture is pretty bleak. We're all going to kill ourselves eventually. That's why the 'Save the Humans' slogan of the Turner Foundation is absolutely perfect, because if we save ourselves, we save everything else and vice versa. It all works together."[15]

NOTE: For more on the Turner Foundation, see the section "One Billion at a Time," or log on to the Turner Foundation website at www.turnerfoundation.org.

~

Mother Nature contributes $33 trillion worth of services to humankind each day, according to a report on the Turner Foundation website. Turner left this message on the site, although no doubt it was written for him by someone else. It sounds much too tame for Ted:

"Whether or not the $33 trillion estimate is a completely accurate number, the point is well taken: we cannot ignore the value of the very natural systems on which life depends. We, as shareholders in nature, have an undeniable responsibility in its defense. Imagine a world lacking enough bees, bats, or birds to pollinate our crops or adequate tropical forests to regulate the world's climate or coral reefs to protect our shores. Only nature—natural systems that are strong, vibrant, and healthy—can provide these life sustaining functions."[16]

~

Although Turner is on a crusade to recapture a healthy, whole earth, it is not against his principles to hunt game that is not endangered. After the Goodwill Games in Moscow, Turner took his sons to Botswana on a big-game safari. While the boys simply observed and took photographs, Ted bagged a lion. Later Turner had it stuffed and put on display in the TBS conference room.[17]

At Turner's northern New Mexico spread, Vermejo Park Ranch, hunting is allowed during the legal season. For more about Vermejo see the section, "Give Me Land, Lots of Land."

~

Turner says that in addition to financial support of environmental causes, he does what he can to conserve water:

"I don't always flush. Sometimes I just go out on the front porch and take a whiz on the grass."[18]

GIVE ME LAND, LOTS OF LAND

"I would like to own everything."[19]

⌒

Turner describes himself as a "collector of land."[20]

With well over 1.3 million acres under their control, it is estimated that Ted Turner and Jane Fonda own more property than any other private landholders in the entire United States.

Among other property, the Turner family owns nine ranches in the American West, a 9,000-acre ranch in the picturesque Patagonia region of Argentina, three former rice plantations in the American South, and an island along the lowland coast of South Carolina.

⌒

When cable-TV titan Ted Turner bought his Montana cattle ranch in 1989, his new neighbors suspected the worst motives. They imagined that Turner, who earlier had bought 21,000 acres nearby, might carve up the scenic Rocky Mountain property for ranchettes or perhaps sell part of it to a New Age cult. They also were angered when Turner refused to allow campers to cross his land. Says he: "I bought the place because I wanted to get away from people. We live in an increasingly overcrowded world, and I'm becoming a hermit."[21]

~

Turner says he has no plans to develop the land; rather, he will leave it to the Turner family trust to be maintained as open space. On many of his properties, Turner placed legal restrictions that basically convert them into a series of private wildlife reserves, creating something like a private National Park System. The environmental limitations also have given Turner enormous tax benefits, which critics claim may be a primary motivation for his largesse.[22]

~

Fonda has real estate of her own, including homes in Brentwood and Santa Barbara, California.

~

The Turners' legal residence is in Atlanta, a 700-square-foot apartment atop one of the CNN Center towers. Jane has a 300-square-foot space on the floor below, a giant closet for her clothes. The apartment is in CNN's North Tower, while Ted's office is in the South Tower. He commutes 12 floors down the elevator to the atrium, across an indoor walkway, and then up another 12 floors in the opposite tower.

> *"I've thought about hanging a rope in the middle of CNN Center and swinging across—but if it didn't work ..."*[23]

~

Although Turner Broadcasting System property now belongs to Time Warner, CNN's land holdings were accumulated by Turner. Over the years Turner and CNN have made a significant contribution to the development of downtown Atlanta, and the expansion in Atlanta continues.

"So far this decade, Turner has invested some $400 million downtown in new buildings and sports teams—efforts highlighted by the new Philips Arena, the renovated CNN Center, and Turner Studios, our new television production studio, which will begin operation on January 1, 2000," claimed Turner Properties president Alec Fraser.[24]

In 1985 CNN had outgrown its original studios and offices on Techwood Drive near Georgia Tech University. Turner acquired the Omni towers from a company in bankruptcy. The downtown skyscraper had been a combination amusement park–business complex, and cost Turner $64 million. Although Turner was heavily in debt when he bought the property, the bank that held the mortgage was delighted to have CNN move in, since Atlanta was suffering from urban flight. CNN Center, across from Olympic Park, underwent a $57 million remodeling in 1999. The company also spent $165 million expanding the Techwood Drive campus.

Critics have claimed, however, that Turner received a sweetheart deal on the construction of a new downtown sports arena, since the arena will be formally owned by a local government entity, allowing Turner's sports team to avoid paying property tax.[25]

The Turners also are renovating the historic Glenn Building, which is on Marietta Street between CNN and the Federal Reserve Bank of Atlanta, for their future residence.[26]

~

Turner started his remarkable personal land accumulation with the purchase of the historic Hope rice plantation in 1978. He paid more than $2 million for the estate. Hope is in the South Carolina lowlands, about 40 miles south of Charleston and only 10 miles from Binden, the plantation where, in a fit of despondency, Ed Turner shot himself.

Situated on the banks of the gently flowing Edisto River near the small town of Jacksonboro, Hope covers 5,200 acres of pines, palmettos, and wetlands. All sorts of wildlife, including wild turkeys and alligators, run free in the Turners' woods. Hope also has a white-pillared mansion reminiscent of Tara in *Gone With the Wind*.

In 1985 Dee Woods said that Hope Plantation was Turner's real home. He really relaxed when he went to the plantation: "He is a different person at Hope, even the tone of his voice changes."[27]

From Hope, it is less than a two-hour drive through coastal inlets punctuated with fields of cotton, peanuts, and tomatoes, to the Turners' private St. Phillips Island. St. Phillips is in Gullah Country, across Point Royal Sound from both Parris Island Marine Base and the Hilton Head resort area. The Turners keep several boats at a private landing on St. Helena Island, which they use to reach their secluded retreat. Their island is covered with pine forests and marshes and runs amok with rabbits, raccoons, deer, and other wildlife. There also are several houses on St. Phillips.

～

Turner once owned Kinloch, an estate northeast of Charleston in South Carolina, but his second wife Jane received that plantation in her divorce settlement.[28]

～

The first western ranch Turner acquired was the old Sixteen Mile Ranch near Toston, Montana, halfway between Helena and Bozeman. He renamed the spread Bar None.

Soon afterward, Turner acquired the Flying D Ranch near Gallatin Gateway, a town just south of Bozeman. Turner now owns more than 768,000 acres of ranchland in the Rocky Mountain region.

～

"I'm bringing back the old West, saving key pieces of the world from development. I'm doing it because I enjoy it. It's that simple. At some point I'm going to retire, and I'm a very active person. These ranches

*will give me something pleasurable to do. Besides,
I've always been a collector and the buffalo nickel
was the favorite in my coin collection."[29]*

⌒

The largest landholders in New Mexico, the Turners
own three of the most important ranches in the state.
The 360,000-acre Pedro Armendaris Ranch (acquired
in 1994) includes the entire Fra Cristobal mountain
chain. The 155,000-acre Ladder Ranch near Truth or
Consequences is in the same general region as the
Armendaris. The 580,000-acre Vermejo Park Ranch is
in the far northeastern corner of New Mexico near
Raton.

⌒ ✳ ⌒

VERMEJO PARK RANCH

If any piece of property in the Turner empire repre-
sents Ted Turner's relationship to the earth, it would be
the Vermejo Park Ranch. Vermejo is one of the largest
of the historic land grant ranches, dating back to when
the region still belonged to Old Mexico. Covering 900
square miles, the ranch lies adjacent to the Old Santa Fe
Trail, at altitudes ranging from 6,400 to 13,000 feet. As
with their other places, Turner and Fonda have made a
commitment to leave Vermejo Park Ranch undevel-
oped. The Turners no longer pave the roads, and although
they will allow the existing buildings and improve-
ments to remain, no more will be added.

Like a stately national park without the riffraff, Vermejo Park is the location of New Mexico's oldest hunting lodge. Its historic buildings, many of them constructed from logs, were built and furnished around the beginning of the 20th century. Tiles, fixtures, and furniture were shipped from Europe, usually traveling the final miles to the ranch by mule team. Over the years visitors have included such luminaries as actors Douglas Fairbanks and Mary Pickford, President Herbert Hoover, and industrialist Harvey Firestone.

Although the Turners visit only a few times a year, the Casa Grande adjacent to the main lodge is kept ready for family members. Casa Grande was built in a style called Cowboy Victorian. While a former owner removed many of the antiques, it still contains numerous beautiful pieces of furniture and decorations, including western bronze statues, blown-glass lamps, and a massive grand piano that formerly graced the stage at the Denver Opera House. The home includes seven upstairs bedrooms, a tea room and solarium for the ladies, a bar and smoking lounge for the men, and a massive greenhouse attached to the great ballroom. Jane Fonda is formulating plans to refurbish both Casa Grande and the resort guest rooms.

Most visitors come to Vermejo not for what is found indoors but to experience the great, unspoiled outdoors. Herds of elk, deer, antelope, bighorn sheep, and bison roam the mountain peaks and meadows, and visitors are likely to see black bears grazing in the berry bushes. Wildflowers are abundant, especially at the higher altitudes, where sweeping fields of wild irises bloom each spring.

Vermejo's 21 lakes are stocked with rainbow and

brown trout. Gamekeepers there are striving to return the nearly extinct but indigenous Rio Grande cutthroat trout to the lakes and streams.

Vermejo Park has accommodations for about 75 guests at a time. It includes two small hotel-like buildings, an assortment of cottages, and a larger lodge about 30 minutes away in the mountains. From May to September guests can fly fish in the lakes and streams. In the fall and winter, there are eight elk hunts, including an archery hunt in mid-September. During the fishing season, rates run about $325 per person per night, with a minimum two-night stay. During the hunting season, it can cost up to $10,000 per week. About 85 percent of the hunters bag elk.

The Turner properties are working ranches, and Ted tries to make them financially self-supporting. As a result, Turner owns the largest private herd of bison anywhere.

Turner predicts he can make more money raising bison (commonly called buffalo) than cattle, since bison don't need feeding or winter care and sell for twice the price that cattle do.

"You win on the cost side; you win on the income side. Hell, this could be a business."[30]

182

Cattle were never Turner's favorite creatures anyway. He called them, "Lazy . . . foreign species," and notes that the West would have been better off if cows had never shown up.[31]

~

"Buffalo are . . . better-looking than cows—they don't have fat all over their butts. I want to show you can do something in balance with nature and still make money doing it, twice as much money as you could with cattle."[32]

Turner agrees, however, that cattle are preferable to bison when it comes to dairy products:

"You can't milk [bison], they'll kick your butt."[33]

~

Turner's sons, Teddy Jr. and Beau, help manage the Turner lands. The Turners have attempted to restore the natural plants and animals to the properties and to remove miles and miles of barbed wire fences. Some neighbors in Montana and New Mexico have objected to the Turners' buffalo herds and their environmental management style.

"I don't like all those buffalo out there," complained the barmaid at a Raton hotel. "I don't know why, I just don't."

Beau Turner knows that there are objectors, but, he says, "You can't own this much land and not affect the people living around you. We want to be good neighbors."[34]

~

Sam Donaldson of ABC's *Primetime Live* visited Vermejo Ranch and asked Turner about his plan to be a friend to all creatures, including rattlesnakes.

> Turner: "Rattlesnakes have to have a place to be, too. They can be dangerous. But the danger posed by rattlesnakes, for instance, is minuscule compared to that posed by the automobile."
>
> Donaldson: "Well, people are afraid of snakes in general."
>
> Turner: "I'm afraid of automobiles."
>
> Donaldson: "They also say the snake bites you."
>
> Turner: "Well, the automobile smashes you. You can get so mangled in an automobile accident, they have to scrape you up with a brush and a—with a whisk broom and a—and a dust pan. Whereas a snake, if it bites you, you've got a real good chance, if you can get a doctor, they'll give you some venom and you don't even die."[35]

~

Of his Montana ranch, where Ted and Jane spend most of their time now, Turner says: "I joke that this is my backup life. In case I don't like being vice chairman of Time Warner, I can always come here."[36]

NOTE: For a list of Turner's properties, see "Major Turner Properties" on page 203.

THE QUEST FOR PEACE

Back in the 1970s, Turner thought he had the world figured out:

> *"People who are in love never want to hurt anybody, you know that? It's only horny people who shoot people. If people get all the sex they can handle, they're so happy and content they just sit around and smile. I mean you never feel aggressive just after you've gotten laid, right? Lots of sex for everybody, that's a solution to the world's problems."[37]*

$\sim$

By 1980 Turner was still an advocate of world peace, but he'd grown somewhat more sophisticated:

> *"In the past few years I've changed all my goals. Up until the last few years, I just was enjoying seeing how fast I could go and how much I could accomplish just for the sake of doing it, but it's been in the last two or three years when I got to the position where I met a lot of our leaders and I've asked them questions and I've done a lot of reading and I'm really concerned about our country and our world, so I've kind of come up a do-gooder rather than just trying to rack up personal accomplishments. I'm enjoying it a lot more now—I think I've turned more into a crusader for social progress, for sanity and kindness."[38]*

$\sim$

Turner said his heroes used to be warriors such as Alexander the Great and Napoleon; in 1992 they were people who sought peaceful change, such as Martin Luther King and Gandhi.[39]

~

"Personally, I think that life is very beautiful and it's a real shame that the most intelligent form of life, supposedly, should be building and stockpiling a system that could blow the whole place up."[40]

~

"It's time to stop thinking that other people and countries are foreigners and start thinking of them as neighbors."[41]

~

"I'd like to see a world without land mines, with kids out playing. I'd like to see us act like highly educated, civilized human beings."[42]

~

Gun control may not be the answer to peaceful living, Turner said: "I have a small arsenal myself because I hunt. I don't think outlawing guns is the answer. I think we should outlaw their use on each other. I'm not against guns for armies. Single-shot rifles. I'm against bombs and nuclear arms. I think it's crazy to drop bombs on cities. I believe the wars should be fought between soldiers out in the field. Like at Waterloo and Gettysburg, where you just go out and knock around."[43]

＊

"What we need is a Big Daddy to take us behind the woodshed and take a big board and hold us by the ankles and give it to us good."[44]

＊

When he met with Mikhail Gorbachev during the Goodwill Games, Turner told the Soviet premier:

"I see myself as a citizen of the earth. I don't want to see any nuclear weapons going off over your country or over my country. Those are short-term victories. Those victories only last twenty-four or forty-eight hours. If we bomb you, it's gonna hurt us. And if you bomb us, it's gonna hurt you. Look, I have kids, you have kids. What's their future gonna be like?"[45]

＊

"So I said to Gorbachev, you should take the lead in disarmament. . . . Of course, he didn't thank me when he won the Nobel Prize."[46]

ONE BILLION AT A TIME

When Turner disclosed to Jane Fonda his plan to donate $1 billion to the United Nations for peaceful uses, she cried with joy, then asked if he'd called the lawyers. He said he had but added, "I've already made up my mind."

"He told me several times," said Jane, " 'This is too scary, I'm giving away a third of what I'm worth.'"[47]

At the cocktail party just before Turner announced his unexpected gift to the U.N., he talked to his good friend Vartan Gregorian, president of the Carnegie Corporation.

"Tell me," he said to Gregorian, "You're a big fund raiser. What's the largest gift ever?"

Gregorian said that it was likely to be Walter Annenberg's $500 million contribution to educational causes.

"I'm going to give a billion tonight," said Turner sounding a little uncertain.

"He was building momentum, testing the propellers," explained Gregorian.[48]

After he made the announcement regarding the donation, Turner's butterflies seemed to settle:

"You know, it's not easy to give up your hard-earned money, but once you do, you really feel wonderful. I just hope this giving thing is contagious."[49]

Turner then declared: "I'm putting every rich person in the world on notice. They're going to be hearing from me about giving money away. If you want to lead, you got to get out front and lead—you got to blow the horn and get out in front of the parade. There is no greater joy in life than giving to worthy causes."[50]

~

Turner has difficulty understanding people like Warren Buffett, the billionaire chairman of Berkshire Hathaway Inc., who put most of their wealth in a trust to be distributed after their death:

"I know a lot of these super rich—probably a third of the really rich people in this country. Warren [Buffett] is worth $20 billion. I said, 'Warren, it's great to give all your money to overpopulation, but if you live another 20 years, the world's going to double in that time. You wouldn't miss a billion.' He probably doesn't spend anything. He stays at home every night and plays bridge on the Internet with friends in other parts of the country."[51]

Turner told a reporter that Microsoft founder Bill Gates and Buffett said they would give more to charity if they got more publicity for it. Warren Buffett bristled at the comment: "I never had such a conversation with Turner or with anyone else."[52]

~

Thanks to the U.N. contribution, Turner rose on the largest-donors list but slipped lower on the list of wealthiest Americans.

"My hand shook when I signed the papers [for the U.N. donation], because I knew I was taking myself out of the running for the richest man in America."[53]

~

"That [Forbes Four Hundred] list is destroying our country. These new super rich won't loosen up their wads because they're afraid they'll reduce their net worth and go down on the list."[54]

~

Turner has admired George Soros's efforts to help establish world peace by empowering individuals in strife-torn nations.[55]

~

Turner later became chairman of the United Nations Foundation and in 1999 earmarked $1 million to support U.N. relief efforts in Kosovo, a southern province of Serbia under attack by its own government. The grant was used to provide shelter, blankets, and other necessities for refugees.[56]

~

The United Nations is not the only organization that Turner has helped. He serves on the board of the Martin Luther King Center for Nonviolent Changes, the Greater Yellowstone Coalition, and the International Founders Council of the Smithsonian Museum of the American Indian. He is on the advisory council for the Nuclear Age Peace Foundation. Others who have served on the council are Dr. Helen Caldicott, Jean-Michel Cousteau, Daniel Ellsberg, the 14th Dalai Lama, former New Zealand Prime Minister David Lange, Elisabeth Kübler-Ross, Bishop Desmond Tutu, and several retired U.S. generals and admirals. Linus Pauling and Carl Sagan also served on the committee.

～

In 1994 Turner announced he would be giving $75 million in three chunks of $25 million each to the schools he attended, McCallie School in Chattanooga, Tennessee, and Brown University, and his son's alma mater, the Citadel. The gifts were made in a combination of cash and shares of Turner Broadcasting (later Time Warner), which were placed in a trust.[57]

Turner's financial advisors suggested he maintain the flexibility of designating the amount of money that went to various schools. That way, if something changed at one of the institutions that Turner didn't like, he could adjust his gift accordingly. Turner reacted quickly.

"Absolutely not! That's like Indian giving!"[58]

～

"There are a lot of people who are awash in money they don't know what to do with. It doesn't do you any good if you don't know what to do with it."[59]

～

"I have learned—the more good that I did, the more money comes in."[60]

～

The Turner Family Foundation was formed in 1991 and is run by a former head of Greenpeace USA. All of Turner's children serve on the board of directors.[61]

On the topic of trust funds, Teddy Turner says, "I can take credit for having inspired Dad a little bit. I think he saw that we didn't know how to spend it, to work with the newfound wealth in our trust funds. I think it actually was a wake-up call to him, you know, 'If I pass away and give my kids money, what will they do with it? It will probably just be spent.'"[62]

~

Jennie Turner Garlington says of her father, "I think as he gets older, there is a greater feeling of urgency in him. You can't wait to do something, he's saying. There's no time to wait."[63]

~

Some Atlantans claim that despite Turner's generosity to good causes worldwide, he has neglected Atlanta, which has its own share of poverty and need. About 20 percent, or $2.7 million, of the Turner Foundation's donations in 1997 went to groups doing good works in Atlanta.[64]

~ ✳ ~

SOME TURNER CHARITIES

Asked which charities he favored, Turner replied:

"All of them. I'm also concerned about the threat of nuclear war, overpopulation, soil erosions, acid rain, endangered species, bigotry, snobbery, hatred of war, all of those things. As well as disease, hunger and lack of education. I worry about the ozone layer and oil spills. . . ."[65]

The Turner Foundation has given grants to National Public Radio, the National Museum of the American Indian, the Center for Environmental Citizenship, and Arizona State University for archaeological excavations in New Mexico, Advocates for Youth, American Association for the Advancement of Science, the Georgia Campaign for Adolescent Pregnancy Prevention, the National Audubon Society, and Planned Parenthood, among dozens of other organizations. The following list is extensive, but it is not complete, because older grants may have expired and new grants are continually being added:

Antarctica Project

Campaign for Courageous: Turner donated $10,000 to the campaign to restore the two-time America's Cup–winning yacht.

Civil War Battlefields Preservation

Community Youth Development Initiative: $800,000 in grants for 17 rural communities near Turner properties in Montana, Nebraska, New Mexico, and South Carolina

Corporation for Olympic Development in Atlanta

Great Bear Foundation: A Montana group that works to preserve British Columbia wilderness for native bear population

Love Canal/Center for Health, Environment, and Justice: Works with 8,000 grass-roots groups to clean up toxic waste sites

Physicians for Social Responsibility

Russian Environmental Law Project

The SuperChallenge: Goodwill Games will donate $1 for
every hour volunteered nationally to Atlanta-based
Boys & Girls Clubs of America (1997)

Trees Atlanta

Turner Endangered Species Fund[66]

~ ✳ ~

TED FOR PRESIDENT—NOT!

In 1978 Turner disclosed:

> *"I've thought about being President, but I've got
> to do something else first—like be a governor or a
> Senator—to learn the job."*[67]

~

In 1980 Turner told former business associate Irwin
Mazo that he had four great ambitions:

"One, I'm going to make Channel 17 [WTBS] the
fourth national network. Two, I'm going into the production business—they're producing trash on movies
and TV. Three, I am going to be this country's wealthiest man. And four, I am going to be president of the
United States."

Mazo said, "How can you be president? You have
no political base."

"I've got the boob tube. If this country falls flat on its face, I can go on the boob tube. That's power."[68]

～

In 1986 Turner said: "I would only run for president if it was the only way I could get this country to turn around. My main concern is to be a benefit to the world, to build up a global communications system that helps humanity to come together, to control population, to stop the arms race, to preserve the environment. I'm a deep thinker. I've traveled all over. I have more access to information than anyone on the planet."[69]

～

According to *The Atlanta Constitution*, the Georgia media mogul was the top choice of some Southern power brokers to be a third-party candidate in 1992, but the group turned to Ross Perot after deciding Turner's use of lithium for a mood disorder (which Turner says was misdiagnosed) would be a liability.[70]

～

Approached in 1999 about running for the presidency, Turner said: "I'm thinking about it. It's too early."[71]

～

What kind of politician would Turner be? In 1978 he described himself this way: "I'm conservative fiscally and a liberal socially. I'd take care of welfare by making everybody work who could. Some hard labor, like digging ditches, for the minimum wage."[72]

~

In 1980 Turner expressed strong views on national spending priorities:

"I think that we need to cut out the social programs. We have just been insane with these social and welfare programs, where we've given people that are perfectly capable of working the money to stay at home and watch TV all day. Your and my tax money is being taken to support thousands and thousands of people who are just sitting on their behinds doing nothing when that money should have been spent in national defense."[73]

~

As he grew older and better informed, some of Turner's concepts changed. Fundamentally though, he remains a fiscal conservative and a social liberal:

"You can have a free nation only if the majority of the people are intelligent enough to vote to preserve their freedom. You just can't go out as we are doing at the present time and continue to vote yourself benefits that the society can't pay for. You can't keep operating at the deficits that we are piling up. You can't have 10 percent of your population unemployed and expect to be around very long before you have a revolution."[74]

~

"Capitalism and democracy are the hardest systems to set in working order, and of all the governments that have existed since time began, probably the rarest form of government was democracy and capitalism—the very rarest. It has advantages and disadvantages and it normally doesn't last very long because when people run the country rather than one or two or a small group of people, you have to be intelligent, hard working and be able to make sacrifices. Otherwise, it doesn't work and that's what we are seeing here. We are seeing our form of government disappearing from the face of the earth right now."[75]

~

Turner used the automobile industry as an example of why the U.S. democracy is not working as well as it used to:

"They [the automobile industry in 1980] got fat and lazy and complacent, didn't look ahead. Look at the American cars—slam the door and the door falls off, then the plastic falls off the door. The work ethic is gone in this country. Everybody is ripping everybody else off—we're voting for whoever promises the most, you know, inflation—we're getting exactly what we deserve."[76]

~

"He doesn't have specific politics," said an Atlanta political analyst, "just very strong beliefs."[77]

"I'm not sure whether I'm a liberal conservative or a conservative liberal . . . I mean, nobody wants to die. Everybody loves their mother and father . . . I think this liberal/conservative thing is overstated. We're all people first."78

∼

Turner suggested that maturity and politics make a good combination:

"We've got to begin turning to our tribal elders for advice and strategy. We need to combine gray hair with the look of hemorrhoids because it could be political dynamite."79

∼

Jane Fonda has objected to Turner's political ambitions, saying that she was married to one politician, and once was enough.

"I am very serious about running for president, but Jane doesn't want me to do it."80

Whether he ever becomes president or not, Turner has a vision of what the United States is, or should be:

"America has a mission. It was created by the rest of the world for a special reason. We are an instrument to provide leadership. Your job, all of you in this room, is to create the next generation of American eagles who will live all over the world."81

LIFE IS NICE

"I want to live five lives. I have to hurry to get them all in."[1]

~

Ted Turner has led many lives, but even as he enters his seventh decade, he keeps reinventing himself:

"My father always said to never set goals you can reach in your lifetime. After you accomplish them, there's nothing left."[2]

~

Turner puts good fortune into an interesting perspective:

"I mean, you have to realize how lucky you are that you weren't born a mosquito. Not to mention people—a black guy wonders, why wasn't I born white? Or a guy from India says, why wasn't I born an American? But you're still better off than a mosquito, 'cause it lives only one summer and gets swatted at every time it gets a bite to eat."[3]

~

In an interview with *Saturday Evening Post*, Turner was asked, "Given your choice of anyone in history, what person would you most like to be?" His answer:

"Who in history would I most like to be? That's easy. Ted Turner."

The interviewer asked, "You mean there's no one in all of history you'd rather be?"

"No," responded Turner, "I'm in history, and I like myself. I wouldn't want to be anyone else."[4]

∿

Turner's view of himself in time and place gives him a certain immunity from criticism:

"I don't care what people say about me, I'm too busy making history."[5]

∿

Whatever the future holds for Ted Turner, he has lived passionately thus far. Living life to the maximum is what it's all about for Turner. When he won the arduous Sydney-to-Hobart yacht race by a few boat lengths and a protest, Turner quoted from Joseph Conrad's *Nigger of the Narcissus*:

"Ah, the good old time—the good old time. Youth and the sea. Glamor and the sea! The good, strong sea, the salt, bitter sea, that could whisper to you and roar at you and knock your breath out of you.

"By all that's wonderful it is the sea, I believe, the sea itself—or is it youth alone? Who can tell? But you here—you all had something out of life: money,

*love—whatever one gets on shore—and, tell me,
wasn't that the best time, that time when we were
young at sea: young and had nothing, on the sea that
gives nothing, except hard knocks—and sometimes a
chance to feel your strength—that only—that you
all regret?*

"*The crew of the* American Eagle *drifted out of
sight. I never saw them again. The sea took some, the
steamers took others, the graveyards of the earth will
account for the rest. So be it! Let the earth and the
sea each have its own.*

"*A gone shipmate, like any other man, is gone
forever; and I never saw one of them again. But at
times the spring-flood of memory sets with force up
the dark river of the nine bends. Then on the waters
of the forlorn stream drifts a ship—a shadowy ship
manned by a crew of shades. They pass and make a
sign, in a shadowy hail. Haven't we, together and
upon the immortal sea, wrung out a meaning from
our sinful lives? Good-bye brothers! You were a good
crowd. As good a crowd as ever fisted with wild cries
the beating canvas of a heavy foresail; or tossing
aloft, invisible in the night, gave back yell for yell to
a westerly gale.*"[6]

Ted may have some excellent memories, but the present also makes him happy:

"*Life is nice, particularly if you have your own
plane and your own baseball team.*"[7]

～

"If you live long enough, you're going to get old. You know, I certainly feel like I've slowed up just a little bit."[8]

～

"Years ago, I came up with what I was going to say to an assassin if he came to shoot me. You want to know what it is? 'Thanks for not coming sooner.' Pretty good, huh?"[9]

～

Turner has chosen the epitaph for his tombstone: "I have nothing more to say."[10]

PROPERTY	SIZE	PURCHASED	COST	COMMENTS
MONTANA				
Flying D Ranch *(near Bozeman, Gallatin Gateway)*	107,000 acres	1989	$20 million	5,700 bison, 4,000 elk
Snowcrest Ranch	26,000 acres	1993		800 bison
Bar None Ranch *(between Helena and Bozeman)*	24,000 acres	1987		Dinosaur Fossils
Red Rock River Ranch	5,000 acres	1996		Fishing
NEW MEXICO				
Vermejo Park Ranch *(near Raton)*	588,000 acres	1996	$80 million	2,500 bison, 10,000 elk, 22 lakes 30 miles of fishing streams
Armendaris Ranch *(on Elephant Butte Reservoir)*	360,000 acres	1994		1,900 bison, 700 antelope.
Ladder Ranch *(near Truth or Consequences)*	155,000 acres	1992		2,100 bison, 500 elk.

MAJOR TURNER PROPERTIES

PROPERTY	SIZE	PURCHASED	COST	COMMENTS
NEBRASKA				
Spikebox Ranch (*Western Nebraska*)	40,000 acres	1995		1,800 bison
SOUTH CAROLINA				
Hope Plantation (*near Charleston*)	5,000 acres	1978	$2 million	Former Rice Plantation
St. Phillips Island (*near Hilton Head*)	5,000 acres	1979		Private Island
FLORIDA				
Avalon (*east of Tallahassee*)	8,100 acres			Plantation
ARGENTINA				
Patagonia	9,000 acres			Wilderness Ranch

TIMELINE

1937 Jane Seymour Fonda, Turner's third wife, was born on December 21 in New York City.

1938 *November 19:* Edward Robert Turner III (Ted) was born in Cincinnati, Ohio, to Edward Turner and Florence Rooney Turner.

1947 The Turner family moved to Savannah, Georgia.

Ted was enrolled in the Georgia Military Academy.

1948 Turner's father transferred him to McCallie, a Christian/military school in Chattanooga, Tennessee.

1956 Turner won the Champion Tennessee Affirmative Team, debating champions.

He graduated from McCallie.

Turner entered the International Lightning Regatta in Canada, coming in 26th place.

Rejected by Harvard, Turner enrolled at Brown University.

1957 Turner's parents, Ed and Florence, were divorced.

Ted pledged the Kappa Sigma fraternity at Brown University.

1958 *February 12:* Turner enlisted in the U.S. Coast Guard during a semester-long suspension from Brown University.

1960 Turner, with his fiancée Judy Nye as crew, won the Y-Flyer National sailing race.

Julia Gayle Nye and Robert Edward Turner III were married at St. Chrystsostom's Episcopal Church in Chicago on June 22. (Some records say June 23.)

December 15: Mary Jane, Ted's 19-year-old sister, died of lupus erythematosis.

At age 22, Ted Turner became general manager of Turner Advertising Company's Macon, Georgia branch.

1961 In July, the Turners' daughter, Laura Lee, was born.

1963 Ed Turner, Ted's father, committed suicide.

Ted and his wife Judy separated. In May, Robert Edward Turner IV was born.

1964 Turner teamed with sailing friend Andy Green and attempted to qualify for the U.S. Olympic team. They qualified for the 5.5-meter finals but were placed seventh and eliminated.

June 2: Turner married his second wife, Jane Shirley Smith, in Birmingham, Alabama.

1966 Ted Turner, sailing *Vamp X*, won the Southern Ocean Racing Circuit (SORC) series by the largest margin in history.

1970 Turner acquired WJRJ, Channel 17, an Atlanta UHF station. He changed its call letters to WTCG (Turner Communications Group), and it eventually became the Atlanta Superstation.

Turner was named Yachtsman of the Year for the first time and presented with the Martini & Rossi trophy.

1971 Turner's *American Eagle* set a course record in the Fastnet Race off the coast of Great Britain.

Turner won the World Ocean Racing Cup in Australia.

1972 Turner took first place in the Sydney-Hobart regatta.

1973 Sailing *Lightnin'*, Turner again won the SORC.

For the second time, Turner was named Yachtsman of the Year.

1974 *November 1:* Turner was inducted into the Brown University Athletic Hall of Fame.

Turner entered the America's Cup Yacht race but was eliminated early.

1976 *January 6:* At a press conference, Turner announced that he'd bought the Atlanta Braves baseball team. The team was last place in its league.

December 17: Channel 17 in Atlanta, the satellite television Superstation, went on the air.

1977 Bowie Kuhn, baseball commissioner, suspended Turner from baseball for one year as punishment for his radical behavior as a baseball team owner.

Turner successfully defended a challenge to the America's Cup yacht race sailing *Courageous*.

For the third time, Turner was named Yachtsman of the Year.

Turner purchased the Atlanta Hawks basketball team.

1978 Turner acquired Hope Plantation, a beautiful estate about 40 miles south of Charleston, South Carolina.

Turner made his second appearance before the Van Deerlin U.S. House of Representatives subcommittee that was rewriting the 1934 Communications Act.

December 6: At 8:35 P.M., RCA's *Satcom III*, which Turner had booked to beam the aborning CNN to cable companies, disappeared shortly after launch. Turner was left without a satellite for his biggest television venture.

For the fourth time, Turner was named Yachtsman of the Year.

Turner and sailor Gary Jobson co-wrote *The Racing Edge: Sailing Techniques, Tactics and Philosophy of the America's Cup Skipper and His Tactician* (Simon & Schuster).

Turner won Britain's Fastnet race, in which 23 competitors died and 44 boats were either sunk or damaged in a ferocious storm.

1980 Turner participated in the SORC and later that year made an unsuccessful bid in the America's Cup race.

June 1: Cable News Network (CNN), headquartered in Atlanta, took to the airwaves.

1981 *May 11:* CNN sued ABC, CBS, NBC, President Ronald Reagan, White House Chief of Staff James Baker, and Deputy Press Secretary Larry Speaks for violating CNN's equal rights to access to the news when network reporting pools were created and CNN was left out. Secretary of State Alexander Haig later was added to the suit.

1982 *February 12:* Ted Turner and a CNN crew flew to Havana as a guest of Fidel Castro. Castro and Turner went duck hunting.

Also in February, CNN employees rejected unionizaton by a 156 to 53 vote.

After six years of poor showings, the Atlanta Braves won the National League West pennant.

1983 Turner bought a competing headline news cable network, Satellite News Channel, for $25 million and then closed it down.

Turner won the Sydney-Hobart yacht race in a very close heat, only after protesting that another boat failed to give his boat its proper right of way.

1984 The Cable Music Channel debuted. The venture was shut down a month after it started and its assets were sold to MTV for $1 million.

1985 *April:* Turner announced a hostile takeover bid for the CBS television network. After several unsuccessful attempts to raise the necessary funds, Turner gave up.

Kirk Kerkorian, majority shareholder of Metro-Goldwyn-Mayer/United Artists, contacted Turner. The two worked out a deal for TBC to acquire MGM/UA for $1.5 billion.

1986 *March 25:* Turner completed the purchase of MGM/UA, a deal that in the beginning nearly bankrupted Turner but, in time, vastly increased his wealth.

June 6: Turner was forced to sell part of MGM/UA back to Kirk Kerkorian, the original owner.

July 5–July 20: The first Goodwill Games were held in Moscow, Russia.

1987 *June 3:* A group of cable companies bought a 37 percent stake in Turner Broadcasting System for $652.5 million, bailing Turner out from the overwhelming debt of the MGM/UA purchase. Turner lost control of TBS, although he remained head of the company, a board member, and a major owner.

Ted and Jane Smith Turner were divorced. Janie reportedly received a settlement estimated at between $18 million to $20 million. Over a short time, the settlement is said to have escalated to a value of $40 million.

Ted Turner was diagnosed with Epstein-Barr disease, the so-called yuppie chronic fatigue syndrome.

1988 Turner Network Television (TNT), the movie channel, launched operations.

1989 *May:* CNN reporter Bernard Shaw and Beijing bureau chief Mike Chinoy made television history as they covered themselves being thrown off the air during the Chinese Tiananmen Square uprising.

That fall Turner received the prestigious Paul White Award from the Radio-Television News Directors Association, the first entrepreneur to receive the highest honor for broadcast journalism.

1990 The second Goodwill Games were held in Seattle, Washington.

1991 *December 21:* Ted Turner and Jane Fonda were wed in Florida.

Hanna-Barbera, the cartoon company, was acquired by Turner.

The Atlanta Braves made it to the World Series, but lost.

The Turner Family Foundation was created.

1992 *Time* magazine named Turner its Man of the Year.

Florence Turner Carter, Ted's mother, died in Cincinnati at age 82. She had remarried and her second husband was an Ohio businessman.

The Atlanta Braves played in the World Series but again lost.

1993 *August:* Turner acquired New Line and Castle Rock movie production companies.

Brown University, from which Turner was expelled, granted him an honorary doctorate.

1995 The Atlanta Braves won the World Series.

Turner sold his company, TBS, to Time Warner on October 10, 1995, for $2.3 billion in Time Warner stock plus other considerations.

1996   The Braves placed first in their league but lost the World Series.

June 5: Ted Turner was Harvard Law Day speaker.

1997   Turner donated $1 billion to the United Nations for peaceful uses.

1998   The Braves won their seventh straight division title.

Turner and Jane Fonda made a courtesy call on Cuban president Fidel Castro as part of a visit to CNN's Havana office.

1999   Time Warner's Atlanta Thrashers, an expansion ice hockey team, began playing in the new $250 million, 18,500-seat Omni Arena.

TBS announced the formation of a new regional cable channel, Turner South, to serve 6 million cable subscribers in Alabama, Georgia, Mississippi, South Carolina, Tennessee, and North Carolina.

Ted Turner was inducted into the Atlanta Hospitality Hall of Fame in recognition of his help in making Atlanta a tourist attraction.

ENDNOTES

Preface

1. William A. Henry III, "Shaking Up the Networks," *Time*, August 9, 1982, p. 54.

2. Dennis Conner, *No Excuse to Lose* (New York: W.W. Norton & Co., 1978), p. 41.

3. Gwenda Blair, "Once More, With Cheek," *Business Month*, July/August, 1988, p. 33.

4. "Future Talk," *Broadcasting*, May 2, 1988, p. 64.

5. Roger Vaughan, *The Grand Gesture* (Boston: Little, Brown & Company, 1975), p. 23.

6. Ibid., p. 77.

7. Mark Sauer, "Turner Lives Large and Loose," *San Diego Union-Tribune*, October 10, 1998, p. P2.

8. Harry F. Waters, Vincent Coppola, Vernon E. Smith, Cynthia H. Wilson, and Lucy Howard, "Ted Turner Tackles TV News," *Newsweek*, June 16, 1980, p. 66.

Lessons from Sailing

1. Gary Smith, "What Makes Ted Run?" *Sports Illustrated*, June 23, 1986, p. 84.

2. John Rousmaniere, *Fastnet Force 10* (New York: W.W. Norton & Co., 1980), p. 230.

3. Ibid., p. 228.

4. John Skow, "Vicarious Is Not the Word," *Time*, August 9, 1982, p. 57.

5. Ted Turner, BBC Television, August 22, 1979.

6. Geoffrey Miller, "Turner Hopes Disaster Will Promote Safety," *The Atlanta Constitution*, August 17, 1979.

7. Roger Vaughan, *Ted Turner: The Man Behind the Mouth* (Boston: Sail Books Inc., 1978), p. 122.

8. Roger Vaughan, *The Grand Gesture* (Boston: Little, Brown & Company, 1975), p. 96.

9. Jon S. Denny, "Ted Turner Battens Down the Hatches,"*American Film*, July/August 1982, p. 18.

10. Peter Ross Range, "Playboy Interview: Ted Turner," *Playboy*, August 1978, p. 80.

11. Subrata N. Chakravarty, "What New Worlds to Conquer?" *Forbes*, January 4, 1993, p. 87.

12. Gary Smith, "What Makes Ted Run?" *Sports Illustrated*, June 23, 1986, p. 78.

13. Robert Goldberg and Gerald Jay Goldberg, "Citizen Turner," *Playboy*, June 1995, p. 160.

14. Vaughan, *Ted Turner*, p. 77.

15. "Southern Ocean Racing Circuit," *New York Times*, March 30, 1966, p. 46.

16. Atlanta magazine, August 1966, and Vaughan, *The Grand Gesture*, p. 72.

17. Dennis Conner, *No Excuse to Lose* (New York: W.W. Norton & Co., 1978), p. 174.

18. Vaughan, *Ted Turner*, p. 29.

19. Bob Bavier, *The America's Cup: An Insider's View* (New York: Dodd, Mead & Co., 1986), p. 47.

20. Ted Turner and Gary Jobson, *The Racing Edge* (New York: Simon & Schuster, 1979), p. 21.

21. Ibid., p. 28.

22. Porter Bibb, *It Ain't as Easy as It Looks: Ted Turner's Amazing Story* (New York: Crown Publishers, 1993).

23. Vaughan, *The Grand Gesture*, p. 89.

24. Vaughan, *Ted Turner*, p. 34.

25. Vaughan, *The Grand Gesture*, p. 90.

26. Ibid., p. 105.

27. Robert Goldberg and Gerald Jay Goldberg, *Citizen Turner* (New York: Harcourt Brace & Co., 1995), p. 152.

28. Pat Kilpatrick, "Captain of Cable: Ted Turner," *Interview*, September 1980, p. 36.

29. Conner, *No Excuse to Lose*, p. 92.

30. Stephen Steiner, "The Mouth of the South Talks About . . . ." *Sport*, August 1980, p. 18.

31. Ibid.

32. Smith, "What Makes Ted Run?" June 23, 1986, p. 84.

33. Harry F. Waters, Vincent Coppola, Vernon E. Smith, Cynthia H. Wilson, and Lucy Howard, "Ted Turner Tackles TV News," *Newsweek*, June 16, 1980, p. 66.

34. Gwenda Blair, "Once More, With Cheek," *Business Month*, July/August 1988, p. 32.

35. Christian Williams, *Lead, Follow or Get Out of the Way* (New York: Times Books, 1981), p. 13.

36. Goldberg and Goldberg, *Citizen Turner*, p. 160.

214

37. Kilpatrick, "Captain of Cable," p. 37.

38. Vaughan, *Ted Turner*, p. 62.

39. William A. Henry III, "Shaking Up the Networks," *Time*, August 9, 1982, p. 50.

40. Turner and Jobson, *The Racing Edge*, p. 13.

41. Vaughan, *Ted Turner*, p. 227.

42. "Americas Cup,"*Atlanta Constitution*, October 14, 1977, p. D13.

43. Vaughan, *Ted Turner*, p. xvii.

44. Ibid., p. 227.

45. John McNamara, "The Defense: On the Razor's Edge," *Sail*, August 1980, p. 81.

46. Henry, "Shaking Up the Networks," p. 55.

47. Goldberg and Goldberg, *Citizen Turner*, p. 78.

48. Vaughan, *The Grand Gesture*, p. 21.

49. "Ted Turner," *Providence Journal-Bulletin*, May 13, 1986.

50. Curry Kirkpatrick, "Going Real Strawwng," *Sports Illustrated*, August 21, 1986, p. 88.

51. Steiner, "The Mouth of the South," p. 17.

52. James Bates and Elaine Dutka, "Turner's Zigzag Style Is a Merger of Maverick, Mogul," *Los Angeles Times*, August 31, 1995, p. A-20.

53. Ted Jones, *Challenge '77* (New York: W.W. Norton & Company, 1978), p. 183.

54. "No Excuse to Lose," *Newsweek*, August 25, 1980, pp. 54–56.

55. "Ted Turner," *Washington Post*, May 12, 1981.

56. Heard by author, press conference, San Diego, 1987.

57. Ted Turner, "What Yachting Has Meant to Me,"*Yachting*, July 1982, p. 96.

58. Address to the graduates, Georgia State University, 1994, as reported in "The Maxims of Chairman Ted," *Atlanta Magazine*, March 1996, p. 58.

59. Range, "Playboy Interview: Ted Turner," *Playboy*, August 1978, p. 77.

60. Tim Tucker, "'Fun Guy' Turner Relaxes Braves," *Sporting News*, September 6, 1982.

61. Range, "Playboy interview," p. 74.

62. Ibid., p. 77.

A Scared, Scrappy Kid

1. Christian Williams, *Lead, Follow or Get Out of the Way* (New York: Times Books, 1981), p. 20.

2. Ibid., p. 23.

3. Porter Bibb, *It Ain't as Easy as It Looks: Ted Turner's Amazing Story* (New York: Crown Publishers, 1993), p. viii.

4. "The Turners,"*Atlanta Constitution*, July 17, 1970, p. 44.

5. Roger Vaughan, *The Grand Gesture* (Boston, Little Brown, 1975), p. 287.

6. Roger Vaughan, *Ted Turner: The Man Behind the Mouth* (Boston: Sail Books Inc., 1978), p. 155.

7. "Ted Turner Takes New York," *New York*, December 9, 1996, p. 39.

8. Alex Truex,"Surprising Son," *Atlanta Constitution*, May 8, 1977, p. 4D.

9. Priscilla Painton, "The Taming of Ted Turner," *Time*, January 6, 1992, p. 36.

10. Dale Van Atta, "Meet Ted Turner," *Reader's Digest*, Summer 1998, p. 68.

11. Louis J. Salome, "'Naked News': Turner Talks about CNN, War, Dad," *The Atlanta Journal and Constitution*, July 21, 1995, p. P18.

12. "Ted Turner Takes New York," p. 38.

13. Gary Smith, "What Makes Ted Run?" *Sports Illustrated*, June 23, 1986, p. 84.

14. Harry F. Waters, Vincent Coppola, Vernon E. Smith, Cynthia H. Wilson, and Lucy Howard, "Ted Turner Tackles TV News,"*Newsweek*, June 16, 1980, p. 63.

15. "Profile: Ted Turner," *Atlanta Constitution*, May 12, 1973, p. 23.

16. Robert Goldberg and Gerald Jay Goldberg, *Citizen Turner* (New York: Harcourt Brace & Co., 1995), p. 33.

17. Raymonde Alexander, "A Visit with the Turners," *Atlanta Constitution*, January 13, 1976, p. 1B.

18. Mark Curriden, "The McCallie School of Thought," *The Atlanta Journal and Constitution*, April 3, 1994, p. M1.

19. Goldberg and Goldberg, *Citizen Turner*, p. 43.

20. Vaughan, *Ted Turner*, p. 155.

21. Peter Ross Range, "Playboy Interview: Ted Turner," *Playboy*, August 1978, p. 87.

22. "Ted Turner Profile," *Atlanta Constitution*, June 13, 1977, p. 28.

23. Harry F. Waters et al., "Ted Turner Tackles TV News," p. 66.

24. "Playboy Interview: Ted Turner," p. 84.

25. Bibb, *It Ain't as Easy as It Looks*, p. 22.

26. "Playboy Interview: Ted Turner," p. 90.

27. Ted Turner, speech at McCallie School, Chattanooga, Tennessee, January 14, 1993.

28. Goldberg and Goldberg, *Citizen Turner*, p. 38.

29. "Jimmy Brown"*Atlanta Constitution*, August 21, 1979, p. C1.

30. Van Atta, "Meet Ted Turner," p. 204.

31. Simeon Booker, "TV's Ted Turner Reveals Black Man Served as His 'Second' Father," *Jet*, April 18, 1994, p. 54.

32. "Jimmy Brown"*Atlanta Constitution*, August 21, 1979, p. C1.

33. Booker, "TV's Ted Turner Reveals Black Man Served as His 'Second' Father."

34. Ibid.

35. "Ted Turner Profile,"*Atlanta Constitution*, June 13, 1992, p. 28.

36. Maynard Good Stoddard, "Cable TV's Ted Turner: Spirited Skipper of CNN," *The Saturday Evening Post*, March 1984, p. 44.

37. Williams, *Lead, Follow or Get Out of the Way*, p. 16.

38. Goldberg and Goldberg, *Citizen Turner*, p. 56.

216

39. Ibid., p. 59.

40. Ted Turner, Speech at the Salomon Center, April 26, 1995, and Linda Sharaby, "Ted Turner Jokes with Crowd," *The Brown Daily Herald*, April 27, 1995.

41. Bibb, *It Ain't as Easy as It Looks*, p. 28.

42. Vaughan, *The Grand Gesture*, p. 22.

43. From the Brown University *Daily Herald*, October 4, 1957. Reprinted with permission.

44. Vaughan, *Ted Turner*, p. 166.

45. Goldberg and Goldberg, *Citizen Turner*, p. 64.

46. Ibid., p. 77.

47. Vaughan, *The Grand Gesture*, p. 28.

48. Goldberg and Goldberg, *Citizen Turner*, p. 81.

49. Vaughan, *Ted Turner*, p. 127.

50. Turner speech at the Salomon Center.

51. Paul Gray, "Eight Is Not Enough," *Time*, May 14, 1990, p. 25.

52. William A. Henry III, "Shaking Up the Networks," *Time*, August 9, 1982, p. 55.

53. Bibb, *It Ain't as Easy as It Looks*, p. 25.

54. From an interview with David Frost, Goldberg and Goldberg, *Citizen Turner*, p. 90.

55. Tim Powis, "Life at the Top," *McLean's*, June 18, 1990, p. 54.

56. Rebecca Poyner Burns, "The Maxims of Chairman Ted," *Atlanta Magazine*, March 1996, p. 58.

57. Bibb, *It Ain't as Easy as It Looks*, p. 24.

58. Pat Kilpatrick, "Captain of Cable: Ted Turner," *Interview*, September 1980, p. 37.

59. Henry, "Shaking Up the Networks," p. 56.

60. Vaughan, *Ted Turner*, p. 167.

61. Bibb, *It Ain't as Easy as It Looks*, p. 41.

62. Painton, "The Taming of Ted Turner," p. 36.

63. Bibb, *It Ain't as Easy as It Looks*, p. 15.

64. Ted Turner interview by Diane Sawyer, *60 Minutes*, April 20, 1986.

65. Smith, "What Makes Ted Run?" p. 88.

It's Advertising, Stupid

1. Peter Ross Range "Playboy Interview: Ted Turner," *Playboy*, August, 1978, p. 86.

2. Maria Shriver, *First Person*, NBC Telelvision, May 6, 1992.

3. R. E. Turner III, "Leasing: A Key Factor in Operations," *OAAA News*, January 1964, p. 3.

4. Rebecca Poyner Burns, "The Maxims of Chairman Ted," *Atlanta Magazine*, March 1996, p. 58.

5. Charles Haddad, "Ad Executives Love Turner Tales about Old Times and New," *Atlanta Constitution*, March 5, 1999, p. H02.

6. Roger Vaughan, *The Grand Gesture* (Boston: Little, Brown & Company, 1975), p. 100.

7. "Ted Turner Mines the Skies," *Advertising Age*, November 1982, p. B1.

8. Dale Van Atta, "Meet Ted Turner," *Reader's Digest*, September 1998, p. 69.

9. Porter Bibb, *It Ain't as Easy as It Looks: Ted Turner's Amazing Story* (New York: Crown Publishers, 1993), p. 65.

10. Ibid., p. 64.

11. Robert Goldberg and Gerald Jay Goldberg, *Citizen Turner* (New York: Harcourt Brace & Co., 1995), p. 117.

The Brat Who Ate Atlanta

1. Charles Haddad, "Ad Executives Love Turner Tales about Old Times and New," *Atlanta Constitution*, March 5, 1999, p. H02.

2. Ibid.

3. Jon S. Denny, "Interview: Ted Turner," *American Film*, July/August 1982, p. 18.

4. Peter W. Kaplan, "Ted Turner, Station-to-Station," *Esquire*, February 1983.

5. Ibid.

6. Denny, *American Film*.

7. Subrata N. Chakravarty, "What New Worlds to Conquer?" *Forbes*, January 4, 1993, p. 85.

8. Denny, *American Film*.

9. Ibid.

10. Roger Vaughan, *Ted Turner: The Man Behind the Mouth* (Boston: Sail Books Inc., 1978), p. 56.

11. Peter Ross Range "Playboy Interview: Ted Turner," *Playboy*, August 1978, p. 87.

12. Vaughan, *Ted Turner*, p. 107.

13. John N. Ingham and Lynne B. Feldman, *Contemporary American Business Leaders* (Westport, CT: Greenwood Publishing Group Inc, 1990), p. 715.

14. Eleanor Ringel, "With Studio Buys, Turner Crashes Hollywood Club," *The Atlanta Journal and Constitution*, October 3, 1993, p. N01.

15. At a 1993 press conference celebrating the premier of *Gettysburg*; "The Maxims of Chairman Ted," *Atlanta Magazine*, March 1996, p. 58.

16. Chakravarty, "What New Worlds to Conquer?" p. 84.

17. Gwenda Blair, "Once More, With Cheek," *Business Month*, July/August 1988, p. 33.

18. Joseph B. Cumming, Jr., "Ted Turner: 'Captain Outrageous,'" *The Saturday Evening Post*, October 1980, p. 66.

19. Blair, "Once More, With Cheek," p. 30.

20. Furman Bisher, "The Unsinkable Optimist: Turner a One-man World Power," *The Atlanta Journal and Constitution*, July 27, 1994, p. E01.

21. Haddad, "Ad Executives Love Turner Tales," p. H02.

22. "The Rush into Cable TV Is Now Turning into a Retreat," *Business Week*, October 17, 1983, p. 135.

23. William A. Henry III, "Shaking Up the Networks," *Time*, August 9, 1982, pp. 50–51.

24. Maynard Good Stoddard, "Cable TV's Ted Turner: Spirited Skipper of CNN," *The Saturday Evening Post*, March 1984, p. 103.

Seize the Technology

1. James Bates and Elaine Dutka, "Turner's Zigzag Style Is a Merger of Maverick, Mogul," *Los Angeles Times*, August 31, 1995, p. A20.

2. Harry F. Waters, Vincent Coppola, Vernon E. Smith, Cynthia H. Wilson, and Lucy Howard, "Ted Turner Tackles TV News," *Newsweek*, June 16, 1980, p. 66.

3. Subrata N. Chakravarty, "What New Worlds to Conquer?" *Forbes*, January 4, 1993, p. 86.

4. Waters et al. "Ted Turner Tackles TV News," p. 61.

5. Ibid., p. 59.

6. Pat Kilpatrick, "Captain of Cable: Ted Turner,"*Interview*, September 1980, p. 37.

7. Ibid., p. 36.

8. Waters et al., "Ted Turner Tackles TV News," p. 59.

9. "Turner Vows Worldwide CNN as Cable's Coming Tops Edinburgh Agenda," *Variety*, September 8, 1982, p. 96.

10. William A. Henry III, "Shaking Up the Networks," *Time*, August 9, 1982, p. 51.

11. Louis J. Salome, "'Naked News': Turner Talks about CNN, War, Dad," *The Atlanta Journal and Constitution*, July 21, 1995, p. P18.

12. Waters et al., "Ted Turner Tackles TV News."

13. Henry, "Shaking Up the Networks," p. 52.

14. Geraldine Fabrikant, "Ted (Don't Fence Me In) Turner," *The New York Times*, November 24, 1996.

15. Waters et al.,"Ted Turner Tackles TV News," p. 63.

16. David Carey, "The Confessions of Ted Turner," *Financial World*, April 18, 1989, p. 63.

17. Henry, "Shaking Up the Networks," p. 56.

18. Harry F. Waters, "On the Trail of Tears," *Newsweek*, October 10, 1994, p. 56.

19. Ibid.

20. Jeffrey Scott, "Geronimo," *The Atlanta Journal and Constitution*, December 2, 1993, p. E1.

21. Jeff Peline, "Turner, Ellison Debut Custom News," *CNET News.com*, June 4, 1997.

22. Ibid.

23. Ibid.

A Sports Empire

1. Maynard Good Stoddard, "Cable TV's Ted Turner: Spirited Skipper of CNN," *The Saturday Evening Post*, March 1984, p. 44.

2. Mark Sauer, "Turner Lives Large and Loose," *The San Diego Union-Tribune*, October 10, 1998, p. P2.

3. Roger Vaughan, *Ted Turner: The Man Behind the Mouth* (Boston: Sail Books Inc., 1978), p. 41.

4. Ibid., p. 47.

5. Peter Ross Range "Playboy interview: Ted Turner," *Playboy*, August, 1978, p. 77.

6. "Not the Government's Fault," *Atlanta Constitution*, January 14, 1976, p. 34.

7. Vaughan, *Ted Turner*, p. 277.

8. "Phil Neikro Victory," *Atlanta Constitution*, April 21, 1976, p. D4.

9. "The Little Guy's Hero," *Atlanta Constitution*, April 5, 1976.

10. Vaughan, *Ted Turner*, p. xvii.

11. Ibid., p. 83.

12. Ibid., p. 42.

13. Bob Hope, "Ted Tampers His Way to a Summer's Sail," *The Atlanta Journal and Constitution*, June 18, 1991, p. B3.

14. Robert Goldberg and Gerald Jay Goldberg, *Citizen Turner* (New York: Harcourt Brace & Co., 1995), p. 193.

15. Ted Turner, Comments to Baseball Commissioner Bowie Kuhn, 1977, as reported in "The Maxims of Chairman Ted," *Atlanta Magazine*, March 1996, p. 58.

16. Kent Hannon, "Benched from the Bench," *Sports Illustrated*, May 23, 1977, p. 68.

17. Vaughan, *Ted Turner*, p. 36.

18. Rebecca Poyner Burns, "The Maxims of Chairman Ted," *Atlanta Magazine*, March 1996, p. 58.

19. Ken Picking, "Turner Is Cleared of Tampering," *The Sporting News*, December 6, 1980, p. 51.

20. Bill Conlin, "Kuhn Tragedy: Vetoes Without Reasons," *The Sporting News*, November 15, 1982, p. 43.

21. Tucker, "'Fun Guy' Turner Relaxes Braves," p. 41.

22. Ibid.

23. Stephen Steiner, "The Mouth of the South Talks About ..." *Sport*, August 1980, p. 18.

24. Harry F. Waters, Vincent Coppola, Vernon E. Smith, Cynthia H. Wilson, and Lucy Howard, "Ted Turner Tackles TV News," *Newsweek*, June 16, 1980, p. 63.

25. Steiner, "The Mouth of the South Talks About ..." *Sport*, August 1980, p. 18.

26. Range, "Playboy Interview: Ted Turner," *Playboy*, August 1978, p. 70.

27. Tim Tucker, "A Game, Not War," *The Sporting News*, October 31, 1981, p. 45.

28. Tim Tucker, "Turner and Jax Buddies Forever," *The Sporting News*, January 9, 1982, p. 42.

29. Tim Tucker, "Braves Sure Bet Says Seer Turner," *The Sporting News*, April 3, 1982, p. 45.

30. Ibid.

31. "Rags to Riches," *The Sporting News*, October 11, 1982, p. 45.

32. Ibid.

33. Gary Smith, "What Makes Ted Run?" *Sports Illustrated*, June 23, 1986, p. 84.

34. Steiner, "The Mouth of the South Talks About," p. 17.

35. Ibid., p. 18.

36. Ibid., p. 17.

37. Randall Poe, "Talk Isn't Cheap," *Across the Board*, September 1992, p. 21.

38. Jason Zweig, "Ted Turner and El Gigante," *Forbes*, July 9, 1990, p. 106.

39. Subrata N. Chakravarty, "What New Worlds to Conquer?" *Forbes*, January 4, 1993, p. 85.

40. Joseph B. Cumming, Jr., "Ted Turner: 'Captain Outrageous,'" *The Saturday Evening Post*, October 1980, p. 64.

41. "In Their Own Words," *The Atlanta Journal and Constitution*, February 17, 1993.

42. "The Goodwill Games," *The Wall Street Journal*, July 3, 1986.

43. Goldberg and Goldberg, *Citizen Turner*, p. 367.

44. "Turner's Goodwill Games," *The Wall Street Journal*, July 8, 1986.

45. Goldberg and Goldberg, *Citizen Turner*, p. 374.

46. Ibid., p. 370.

47. Furman Bisher, "The Unsinkable Optimist: Turner a One-Man World Power," *The Atlanta Journal and Constitution*, July 27, 1994, p. E1.

The Next Big Thing

1. Rebecca Poyner Burns, "The Maxims of Chairman Ted," *Atlanta Magazine*, March 1996, p. 58.

2. Roger Vaughan, *Ted Turner: The Man Behind the Mouth* (Boston: Sail Books Inc., 1978), p. 45.

3. Howard Rudnitsky, "The Mouth of the South Strikes Again," *Forbes*, November 7, 1983, p. 82.

4. David Carey, "The Confessions of Ted Turner," *Financial World*, April 18, 1989, p.64.

5. Anita Sharpe, "Turner's New Leaf: Trying to Make Do," *Wall Street Journal*, May 9, 1995, p. B1.

6. Don L. Boroughs, "A Media Mogul Moves into the Meat Market," *U.S. News & World Report*, November 14, 1994, p. 108.

7. Sharpe, "Turner's New Leaf," p. B4.

8. Stratford Sherman, "Ted Turner: Back from the Brink," *Fortune*, July 7, 1986, p. 24.

9. Ibid.

10. Robert Goldberg and Gerald Jay Goldberg, "Citizen Turner," *Playboy*, June 1995, p. 157.

11. Ibid., p. 158.

12. Gary Smith, "What Makes Ted Run?" *Sports Illustrated*, June 23, 1986, p. 77.

13. Goldberg and Goldberg, "Citizen Turner," p. 100.

14. Verne Gay, "Managers Take Over TBS Helm," *Advertising Age*, October 6, 1986, p. 1.

15. Sherman, "Ted Turner," p. 24.

16. Penny Pagano, Matt Stump, and Don West, "Neither Broke nor Broken," *Broadcasting*, August 17, 1987, p. 54.

17. Smith, "What Makes Ted Run?" p. 82.

18. Goldberg and Goldberg, "Citizen Turner."

19. Ibid., p. 379.

20. Gwenda Blair, "Once More, With Cheek," *Business Month*, July/August 1988, p. 33.

21. Ibid.

22. Subrata N. Chakravarty, "He's a Constitutional Monarch Now," *Forbes*, September 5, 1988, p. 34.

23. Pagano, Stump, and West, "Neither Broke nor Broken," p. 66.

24. Ibid., p. 50.

25. Sherman, "Ted Turner," p. 24.

26. Ibid.

27. Blair, "Once More, With Cheek," p. 36.

28. Dorothy Rabinowitz, "TV: The Turner Classic Addiction," *The Wall Street Journal*, June 21, 1999, p. A24.

29. Carey, "The Confessions of Ted Turner," p. 65.

30. Harry A. Jessell, "Turner Takes a Swing at Time Warner," *Broadcast & Cable*, October 3, 1994, p. 17.

31. Carey, "The Confessions of Ted Turner," p. 63.

32. Ibid.

33. Eben Shapiro and Jeffrey A. Trachtenberg, "Time Warner's Levin Finally Gets Respect—But at What Price?" *The Wall Street Journal*, September 14, 1995, p. A1.

34. David Carey, "The Confessions of Ted Turner," p. 64.

35. Gary Levin, "Ted Turner Cries Foul at Time Warner," *Advertising Age*, October 3, 1994, p. 2.

36. Goldberg and Goldberg, "Citizen Turner," p. 100.

37. Sharon Churcher, "Information Please: a CBS Lawyer Checks Out Ted Turner," *New York Magazine*, May 13, 1985, p. 13.

38. Gary Levin, "Ted Turner Cries Foul."

39. Ibid.

40. Johnnie L. Roberts, "Ted Turner Wants It Now," *Newsweek*, August 21, 1995, p. 44.

41. Ibid.

42. James Bates and Elaine Dutka, "Turner's Zigzag Style Is a Merger of Maverick, Mogul," *Los Angeles Times*, August 31, 1995, p. A20.

43. Steven Lipin, "Royal Treatment: Mike Milken Will Get a $50 Million Payment for Helping Turner," *The Wall Street Journal*, September 29, 1995, p. A1.

44. Charles Haddad, "'You Only Live Once': Making a Megadeal: Time Warner Has Agreed to Buy Turner Broadcasting, Creating the World's Largest Entertainment Company," *The Atlanta Journal and Constitution*, September 23, 1995, p. B01.

45. Lipin, "Royal Treatment."

46. Marcus Errico, *E! Online News*, October 9, 1996.

47. Elizabeth Lesky, "Ted Turner: 'At Time Warner, We're All Pissed Off,'" *Business Week Online*, February 6, 1997.

48. Ibid.

49. Press Release, Turner Broadcasting Company, "TBS Superstation Confirms December 31 Conversion Date," July 31, 1997.

50. Mark Landler, "3-Way Haggle Is Now Shaping Deal for Turner," *New York Times*, August 31, 1995, p. A1.

51. Bates and Dutka, "Turner's Zigzag Style," p. A1.

52. Jennet Conant, "Married . . . With Buffalo," *Vanity Fair*, April 1997, p. 210.

53. Lesky, "Ted Turner."

54. Meg Carter, "From a Planet to a Satellite," *Independent*, May 12, 1997, pp. 2–3.

The Turner Style

1. Stratford Sherman, "Ted Turner: Back from the Brink," *Fortune*, July 7, 1986, p. 24.

2. Pat Kilpatrick, "Captain of Cable: Ted Turner," *Interview*, September 1980, p. 36.

3. Robert Goldberg and Gerald Jay Goldberg, "Citizen Turner," *Playboy*, June 1995, p. 158.

4. Elizabeth Lesky, "Ted Turner: 'At Time Warner, We're All Pissed Off,'" *Business Week Online*, February 6, 1997.

5. Charles Haddad, "Already 'Fascinating,' Now He's 'Intriguing'," *The Atlanta Journal and Constitution*, December 16, 1995, p. A01.

6. "Ted Turner Takes New York," *New York*, December 9, 1996, p. 38.

7. Subrata N. Chakravarty, "What New Worlds to Conquer?" *Forbes*, January 4, 1993, p. 87.

8. Peter Bart, "Ted Turns Over a New Leaf," *Variety*, September 25–October 1, 1995, p. 9.

9. Geraldine Fabrikant, "Ted (Don't Fence Me In) Turner," *The New York Times*, November 24, 1996, p. F1.

10. Howard Fineman, "Why Ted Gave It Away," *Newsweek*, September 29, 1997, p. 28.

11. Albert Kim, "Ted's Excellent Speaking Engagement," *Entertainment Weekly*, April 21, 1995, p. 15.

12. Sherman, "Ted Turner."

13. Ted Turner, speech at McCallie Military School, January 14, 1993.

14. Kilpatrick, "Captain of Cable."

15. "Ted Turner: Tender-Hearted Tycoon?" *USA Weekend*, November 30, 1997, p. A1.

16. Ibid.

17. Ibid.

18. Harry F. Waters, Vincent Coppola, Vernon E. Smith, Cynthia H. Wilson, and Lucy Howard, "Ted Turner Tackles TV News," *Newsweek*, June 16, 1980, p. 63.

19. Ted Turner, in speech to the American Society of Magazine Editors, February 5, 1997.

20. Sam Donaldson and Diane Sawyer, "Home on the Range," *ABC Primetime Live*, December 10, 1997.

21. Jill Vejnoska, "He's Giving It Away," *The Atlanta Journal and Constitution*, November 16, 1997, p. H1.

22. Peter Ross Range, "Playboy Interview: Ted Turner," *Playboy*, August 1978, p. 90.

23. *Vanity Fair*, October 1995 "New Leaders of the Information Age."

24. Randall Smith, "Turner Shares Down 47% Since June," *The Wall Street Journal*, August 5, 1986, p. 57.

25. Roger Vaughan, *Ted Turner: The Man Behind the Mouth* (Boston: Sail Books Inc., 1978), p. 128.

26. Gary Smith, "What Makes Ted Run?" *Sports Illustrated*, June 23, 1986, p. 76.

27. Ibid.

28. Sherman, "Ted Turner," p. 24.

29. Smith, "What Makes Ted Run?"

30. David Rubinger, "Ted Turner Meets with Fidel Castro as Part of 'Courtesy Visit' to Havana," *Atlanta Business Chronicle*, January 12, 1998.

31. Porter Bibb, *It Ain't As Easy as It Looks: Ted Turner's Amazing Story* (New York: Crown Publishers, 1993), p. 66.

32. Ibid., p. 67.

33. *People*, September 12, 1977, p. 30.

34. Roger Vaughan, *Ted Turner*, 1978, p. 75.

35. Fineman, "Why Ted Gave It Away," p. 28.

36. Mariano Cordero, "El Refugio Natural de Turner y Jane Fonda," *Diario*, September 25, 1997.

The Demon Within

1. Peter Ross Range, "Playboy Interview: Ted Turner," *Playboy*, August 1978, p. 74.

2. Subrata N. Chakravarty, "What New Worlds to Conquer?" *Forbes*, January 4, 1993, p. 87.

3. Priscilla Painton, "The Taming of Ted Turner," *Time*, January 6, 1992, p. 36.

4. Sam Donaldson and Diane Sawyer, "Home on the Range," *ABC Primetime Live*, December 10, 1997.

5. Sam Donaldson, "Ted Turner," *ABC Primetime Live*, December 31, 1997.

6. Robert Goldberg and Gerald Jay Goldberg, *Citizen Turner* (New York: Harcourt Brace & Co., 1995), p. 301.

7. Degen Pener, "Ted's Civil War," *Entertainment Weekly*, November 22, 1996, p. 19.

8. Ibid.

9. Ibid., p. 20.

10. Ibid., p. 22.

11. Nick Taylor, "The American Hero as Media Mogul," *Atlanta*, September 1982, p. 100.

12. Pener, "Ted's Civil War," p. 24.

13. Maynard Good Stoddard, "Cable TV's Ted Turner: Spirited Skipper of CNN," *The Saturday Evening Post*, March 1984, p. 47.

14. Stratford Sherman, "Ted Turner: Back from the Brink," *Fortune*, July 7, 1986, p. 24.

15. "Playboy Interview: Ted Turner," p. 77.

16. Pener, "Ted's Civil War," p. 24.

17. Harry F. Waters, Vincent Coppola, Vernon E. Smith, Cynthia H. Wilson, and Lucy Howard, "Ted Turner Tackles TV News," *Newsweek*, June 16, 1980, p. 66.

18. Dale Van Atta, "Meet Ted Turner," *Reader's Digest*, September 1998, p. 62.

19. Roger Vaughan, *Ted Turner: The Man Behind the Mouth* (Boston: Sail Books Inc., 1978), p. 26.

20. Stoddard, "Cable TV's Ted Turner," p. 44.

21. Vaughan, *Ted Turner*, p. 106.

22. "The Mouth of the South Opens Wide Again, to Change Feet," *The San Diego Union-Tribune*, January 19, 1999, p. D2.

23. Michael Fleming and Timothy M. Gray, "Buzz's Light Year: 101 Damnations," *Variety*, January 6, 1997, p. 1.

24. Goldberg and Goldberg, *Citizen Turner*, p. 208.

25. Vaughan, *Ted Turner*, 1978, p. 24.

26. Ibid., p. 26.

27. Ibid., p. 27.

28. "Defending America's Cup," *Time*, September 19, 1977, p. 84.

29. Porter Bibb, *It Ain't as Easy as It Looks: Ted Turner's Amazing Story* (New York: Crown Publishers, 1993), p. 138.

30. Goldberg and Goldberg, *Citizen Turner*, p. 256.

31. "The Mouth of the South Opens Wide Again."

32. Vaughan, *Ted Turner*, p. 20.

33. "ADL Welcomes Prompt Apology From Ted Turner," Press Release, Anti-Defamation League, July 11, 1992.

34. Richard Zoglin, "The Greening of Ted Turner," *Time*, January 22, 1990, p. 60.

35. Elizabeth Kurylo, "Ted Offers 'I'm Sorry' on China," *The Atlanta Journal and Constitution*, June 13, 1990, p. A1.

36. Ibid.

37. Toby Scott, "Turner Takes Off in China," *Broadcasting & Cable*, August 15, 1994, p. 19.

38. Reuter, Atlanta, "CNN Boss Turner Criticizes TV Viewers, May 10, 1996, AOLNewsProfiles@aol.net.

39. Pat Kilpatrick, "Captain of Cable: Ted Turner," *Interview*, September 1980, p. 36.

40. Randall Poe, "Talk Isn't Cheap," *Across the Board*, September 1992, p. 21.

41. Ted Turner, Speech at the Salomon Center, April 26, 1995.

42. "No One Is Laughing at Ted Now," *Business Week*, April 16, 1984.

43. Sherry Baker, "Ted Turner's Alter Ego," *Atlanta*, April 9, 1985, p. 133.

44. Painton, "The Taming of Ted Turner," p. 37.

45. Waters et al, "Ted Turner Tackles TV News," p. 66.

46. Goldberg and Goldberg, *Citizen Turner*, p. 302.

47. Vaughan, *Ted Turner*, p. 35.

48. Painton, "The Taming of Ted Turner," p. 36.

49. Vaughan, *Ted Turner*.

50. Jennet Conant, "Married . . . With Buffalo," *Vanity Fair*, April 1997, p. 227.

51. Peter Ross Range, "Ted Turner: Playboy Interview," *Playboy*, August 1983, p. 64.

52. Jennet Conant, "Married . . . With Buffalo," p. 224.

Family Values

1. Roger Vaughan, *Ted Turner: The Man Behind the Mouth* (Boston: Sail Books Inc., 1978), p. 128.

2. Address to the 1990 graduating class, Tougaloo College, Jackson, Mississippi.

3. Robert Goldberg and Gerald Jay Goldberg, "Citizen Turner," *Playboy*, June 1995, p. 100.

4. Rebecca Poyner Burns, "The Maxims of Chairman Ted," *Atlanta Magazine*, March 1996, p. 58.

5. *Atlanta Constitution*, March 21, 1992.

6. Porter Bibb, *It Ain't as Easy as It Looks: Ted Turner's Amazing Story* (New York: Crown Publishers, 1993), p. 131.

7. Priscilla Painton, "The Taming of Ted Turner," *Time*, January 6, 1992, p. 37.

8. Bibb, *It Ain't as Easy as It Looks* (New York: Crown Publishers, 1993), p. 144.

9. Goldberg and Goldberg, "Citizen Turner," p. 372.

10. Penny Pagano, Matt Stump, and Don West, "Neither Broke nor Broken," *Broadcasting*, August 17, 1987, p. 66.

11. Ibid., p. 65.

12. Richard Zoglin, "The Greening of Ted Turner," *Time*, January 22, 1990, p. 60.

13. Goldberg and Goldberg, "Citizen Turner."

14. Porter Bibb, *It Ain't as Easy as It Looks*, p. 54.

15. James Dodson, "Teddy Comes About," *Atlanta*, May 1993, p. 108.

16. Gary Smith, "What Makes Ted Run?" *Sports Illustrated*, June 23, 1986, p. 84.

17. Painton, "Taming of Ted Turner," p. 37.

18. Smith, "What Makes Ted Run?" p. 84.

19. Vaughan, *Ted Turner*, p. 83.

20. Maureen Downey, "Teddy Turner's New Challenge Sends Him to the Soviet Union," *Atlanta Constitution*, September 6, 1985, p. C1.

21. Goldberg and Goldberg, "Citizen Turner," June, 1995, p. 374.

22. Mark Sauer, "Turner Lives Large and Loose," *The San Diego Union-Tribune*, October 10, 1998, p. P2.

23. "Ted Turner Takes New York," *New York*, December 9, 1996, p. 39.

24. "Turner & Smooch," *People*, January 27, 1992, p. 40.

25. Howard Fineman, "Why Ted Gave It Away," *Newsweek*, September 29, 1997, p. 28.

26. Jennet Conant, "Married . . . With Buffalo," *Vanity Fair*, April 1997, p. 217.

27. Ibid., p. 227.

28. Ibid.

29. "Remembering Dad," *TV Guide*, January 11, 1992, p. 6.

30. Conant, "Married . . . With Buffalo," p. 230.

31. Ibid.

32. Peter Boyer, "Taking on the World," *Vanity Fair*, April 1991, p. 104.

33. Geraldine Fabrikant, "Ted (Don't Fence Me In) Turner," *The New York Times*, November 24, 1996, p. F1.

34. Conant, "Married . . . With Buffalo," *Vanity Fair*, April 1997, p. 228.

35. Ibid.

36. "Marriage Is Mellowing Jane Fonda," *The Atlanta Journal and Constitution*, September 4, 1992, p. D4.

37. Albert Kim, "Ted's Excellent Speaking Engagement," *Entertainment Weekly*, April 21, 1995, p. 15.

38. Jill Vejnoska, "He's Giving It Away," *The Atlanta Journal and Constitution*, November 16, 1997, p. H1.

39. Ibid.

The Return to Idealism

1. 1993 press conference celebrating the premiere of the TBS documentary *Gettysburg*.

2. Jill Vejnoska, "He's Giving It Away," *The Atlanta Journal and Constitution*, November 16, 1997, p. H1.

3. Pat Kilpatrick, "Captain of Cable: Ted Turner," *Interview*, September 1980, p. 36.

4. Richard Zoglin, "The Greening of Ted Turner," *Time*, January 22, 1990, p. 58.

5. Robert Goldberg and Gerald Jay Goldberg, *Citizen Turner* (New York: Harcourt Brace & Co., 1995), p. 324.

6. Sam Donaldson and Diane Sawyer, "Home on the Range," *ABC Primetime Live*, December 10, 1997.

7. Howard Fineman, "Why Ted Gave It Away," *Newsweek*, September 29, 1997, p. 28.

8. "Turner: Fuel Lack Will Kill Newspapers," *AP*, October 11, 1979, p. 14E.

9. Ted Turner, Speech at the Salomon Center, April 26, 1995.

10. Maynard Good Stoddard, "Cable TV's Ted Turner: Spirited Skipper of CNN," *The Saturday Evening Post*, March, 1984, p. 45.

11. Turner speech at the Salomon Center.

12. Goldberg and Goldberg, *Citizen Turner*, p. 326.

13. Gwenda Blair, "Once More, with Cheek," *Business Monthly*, July/August 1988, p. 38.

14. Vejnoska, "He's Giving It Away."

15. Ibid.

16. "Message from the President," Turner Foundation Inc., www.turnerfoundation.org.

17. Robert Goldberg and Gerald Jay Goldberg, "Citizen Turner," *Playboy*, June 1995, p. 372.

18. Turner speech at the Salomon Center.

19. Goldberg and Goldberg, "Citizen Turner," p. 102.

20. Geraldine Fabrikant, "Ted (Don't Fence Me In) Turner," *The New York Times*, November 24, 1996, p. F1.

21. "Ted's Home on the Range," *Time*, July 31, 1989, p. 41.

22. Goldberg and Goldberg, "Citizen Turner," p. 422.

23. Howard Fineman, "Why Ted Gave It Away," *Newsweek*, September 29, 1997, p. 28.

24. "TBS Leases Space at Centennial Tower," *Atlanta Business Chronicle*, February 15, 1999.

25. Michael Hinkelman, "The Real Dirt behind Hawks Arena Deal," *Atlanta Business Chronicle*, May 12, 1997.

26. Tony Wilbert, "A New Tower for Turner," *Atlanta Business Chronicle*, April 12, 1999.

27. Sherry Baker, "Ted Turner's Alter Ego," *Atlanta*, April 9, 1985, p. 72.

28. Goldberg and Goldberg, "Citizen Turner," *Playboy*, June 1995, p. 386.

29. Charles Haddad, "Vermejo Park Ranch—Ted Turner's Wild West," *The Atlanta Journal and Constitution*, April 11, 1999, p. C1.

30. Don L. Boroughs, "A Media Mogul Moves into the Meat Market," *U.S. News & World Report*, November 14, 1994, p. 108.

31. Ibid.

32. Melissa Turner, "Turner Set to Bull His Way into the Meat Business: He'll Market Buffalo from Montana Ranch," *The Atlanta Journal and Constitution*, September 24, 1991, p. A1.

33. Boroughs, "Media Mogul Moves into the Meat Market."

34. Haddad, "Vermejo Park Ranch Ted Turner's Wild West."

35. Donaldson and Sawyer, "Home on the Range."

36. Fabrikant, "Ted (Don't Fence Me In) Turner," p. F1.

37. Peter Ross Range, "Playboy Interview: Ted Turner," *Playboy*, August 1978, p. 84.

38. Kilpatrick, "Captain of Cable." *Interview*, September 1980, p. 36.

39. Priscilla Painton, "The Taming of Ted Turner," *Time*, January 6, 1992, p. 34.

40. Pat Kilpatrick, "Captain of Cable."

41. Meredith Amdur and Nick Bell, "The Boundless Ted Turner: Road to Globalization," *Broadcasting & Cable*, April 11, 1994, p. 34.

42. Douglas Harbrecht, "Ted Turner on the Superrich, Philanthropy, and the Future," *Business Week Online*, September 26, 1997.

43. Stoddard, "Cable TV's Ted Turner," p. 103.

44. "People," *The New York Times*, July 13, 1986, p. C1.

45. Goldberg and Goldberg, "Citizen Turner," p. 368.

46. Turner speech at the Salomon Center.

47. Fineman, "Why Ted Gave it Away," *Newsweek*, September 29, 1997, p. 28.

48. Ibid.

49. Ibid.

50. Ibid.

51. Harbrecht, "Ted Turner on the Superrich."

52. Robert Lenzner, "The Mouth of the South Puts His Foot In It," *Forbes 400*, October 14, 1996, p.40

53. Ibid.

54. Ibid.

55. Fineman, "Why Ted Gave It Away," p. 28.

56. Norman Kemister and Elizabeth Shogren, "Crisis in Yugoslavia," *The Los Angeles Times*, Wednesday, April 7, 1999, p. A18.

57. Lenzner, "The Mouth of the South."

58. Vejnoska, "He's Giving It Away."

59. "Ted Turner Donates One Billion U.S. Dollars to the United Nations," Nuclear Age Peace Foundation, wagingpeace@napf.org.

60. Ibid.

61. Fineman, "Why Ted Gave It Away," p. 28.

62. Vejnoska, "He's Giving It Away."

63. Ibid.

64. David Rubinger, "Charity Doesn't Begin at Home for Our Complex Native, Turner," *Atlanta Business Chronicle*, October 6, 1997.

65. Stoddard, "Cable TV's Ted Turner," p. 44.

66. Vejnoska, "He's Giving It Away."

67. "Playboy Interview: Ted Turner," p. 90.

68. Gary Smith, "What Makes Ted Run?" *Sports Illustrated*, June 23, 1986, p. 78.

69. Ibid.

70. Don O' Briant, "President Outrageous? Stay Tuned," *The Atlanta Journal and Constitution*, August 6, 1993, p. A1.

71. Bob Dart, "President Ted? Prospect Stirs Debate on Fonda Factor," *Atlanta Constitution*, November 17, 1998, p. A14.

72. "Playboy Interview: Ted Turner," p. 87.

73. Kilpatrick, "Captain of Cable," p. 37.

74. Stoddard, "Cable TV's Ted Turner," p. 103.

75. Pat Kilpatrick, "Captain of Cable."

76. Ibid.

77. Peter Hall, "Ted Turner's Nonevent (His Network Seeing Black)," *Financial World*, April 3, 1985, p. 124.

78. Frederick Allen, "Turner Delights Audience with Self-Inflicted Wounds," July 10, 1985, p. A3.

79. Randall Poe, "Talk Isn't Cheap," *Across the Board*, September 1992, p. 21.

80. Bob Dart, "President Ted? Prospect Stirs Debate on Fonda Factor," *Atlanta Journal Constitution*, November 17, 1998, p. A14.

81. Poe, "Talk Isn't Cheap," p. 21.

Life Is Nice

1. William A. Henry III, "Shaking Up the Networks," *Time*, August 9, 1982, p. 55.

2. "Ted Turner's Marvelous News Machine," *The Economist*, June 21, 1980, p. 30.

3. Peter Ross Range, "Playboy Interview: Ted Turner," *Playboy*, August, 1978, p. 90.

4. Maynard Good Stoddard, "Cable TV's Ted Turner: Spirited Skipper of CNN," *The Saturday Evening Post*, March 1984, p. 44.

5. Jon S. Denny, "Ted Turner Battens Down the Hatches," *American Film*, July/August 1982, p. 18.

6. Joseph Conrad, ed. *Nigger of the "Narcissus"* (New York: W. W. Norton, 1979), pp. 171–172.

7. "Favorite People," *Atlanta Business Chronicle*, February 1, 1999.

8. Sam Donaldson and Diane Sawyer, "Home on the Range," *ABC Primetime Live*, December 10, 1997.

9. Priscilla Painton, "The Taming of Ted Turner," *Time*, January 6, 1992, p. 36.

10. "Favorite People."